"Informative, in? practical insights
"Well done, good obedience and in future self will thank you!"

rewards. Your

LEE STROBEL
New York Times Best-Selling Author

When all is said and done on earth and we stand before our Maker, no greater words could possibly be spoken than "Well done, thou good and faithful servant." *Hearing Jesus Say, "Well Done"* reveals the heart and passion of God—the gospel of our Lord and Savior Jesus Christ.

JENTEZEN FRANKLIN
Senior Pastor, Free Chapel
New York Times Best-Selling Author

Hearing Jesus Say, "Well Done" not only encourages but practically teaches you how to embrace a heavenly perspective, become a bold soul-winner, live an overcoming life, and ensure that you will hear those words we all long for when we get to heaven: "well done." I highly recommend this book for individuals and church groups.

PAULA WHITE-CAIN
President, Paula White Ministries

Dan Steiner is one of the most intense Christians I know. This book reflects his positive passion for life and his ardent desire to hear Jesus say, "Well done!" at life's end. If you've lost your spiritual fervor, read Dan's stimulating book. His spiritual zeal is contagious and will reignite a fresh fire in you.

BOB RUSSELL
Pastor, Bob Russell Ministries

Our life on this earth is only a blip compared to what comes after. Every Christian should be living their life with an eye to eternity, and Dan's excellent book will tell you how.

CHARLIE KIRK
Founder, Turning Point USA
New York Times Best-Selling Author

"Well done" . . . those coveted words we all want to hear from our Lord on that day we stand in His presence. How we live out each moment and opportunity in the days ahead matters. Dan provides heartfelt wisdom and direction in this step-by-step guide to help you one day hear those words. A gift to us all. Until then . . .

TIM CLINTON EdD, LPC, LMFT
President, American Association of Christian Counselors
Executive Director, Liberty University Global Center for Mental Health, Addiction, and Recovery

THE SECRET TO SECURING
HEAVEN'S REWARDS

HEARING JESUS SAY

WELL DONE

DANIEL STEINER

bookVillages

Hearing Jesus Say, "Well Done": The Secret to Securing Heaven's Rewards
Copyright © 2024 by Daniel Steiner

All rights reserved. No part of this publication may be reproduced, stored in a retrieval system, or transmitted in any form by any means, electronic, mechanical, photocopy, recording, or otherwise, without the prior permission of the publisher, except as provided by USA copyright law.

No patent liability is assumed with respect to the use of the information contained herein. Although every precaution has been taken in the preparation of this book, the publisher and author assume no responsibility for errors or omissions. Neither is any liability assumed for damages resulting from the use of the information contained herein.

All Scripture quotations unless otherwise noted are taken from the New King James Version®. Copyright © 1982 by Thomas Nelson. Used by permission. All rights reserved. Scripture quotations marked CSB have been taken from the Christian Standard Bible®, Copyright © 2017 by Holman Bible Publishers. Used by permission. Christian Standard Bible® and CSB® are federally registered trademarks of Holman Bible Publishers. Scripture quotations marked ESV are from the ESV® Bible (The Holy Bible, English Standard Version®), © 2001 by Crossway, a publishing ministry of Good News Publishers. Used by permission. All rights reserved. Scripture quotations marked KJV are taken from the King James Version, public domain. Scripture quotations marked NLT are taken from the Holy Bible, New Living Translation, copyright ©1996, 2004, 2015 by Tyndale House Foundation. Used by permission of Tyndale House Publishers, Carol Stream, Illinois 60188. All rights reserved.

Print ISBN: 978-1-95756-630-6

Cover Design by Bruce Gore, Gore Studio, Inc.
Interior Design by Niddy Griddy Design, Inc.
Interior graphic © iStock

LCCN: 2024917273

Printed in the United States of America

1 2 3 4 5 6 7 8 Printing / Year 29 28 27 26 25 24

*To my Champion, King, and Joy—
Jesus Christ, who has never failed nor forsaken me!*

Contents

Introduction 9

1. A Life That Pleases God 11
2. Well Done, Good and Faithful Servant! 29
3. Your Personal Day Before God 51
4. Your Rewards in Heaven 71
5. To the One Who Overcomes 93
6. Revelation's Secret to Hearing "Well Done" 115
7. Avoiding the Trap 141
8. Faith Vanquishes Fear 163
9. Eternity's Invitation 185
10. The One-Week Challenge 209

Acknowledgments 227
Endnotes 229
About the Author 233

Introduction

If anyone's work which he has built on it endures, he will receive a reward. If anyone's work is burned, he will suffer loss; but he himself will be saved, yet so as through fire.

—1 Corinthians 3:14–15

Your heavenly Father has extravagant love *for* you, belief *in* you, and a desire to *bless* you . . . for an eternity! He wants you to have the best possible life in heaven. That's what this book is about. While the entrance into heaven was purchased without your effort—simply attained by your faith in Jesus—the *experience* of your forever life in heaven is currently being determined by your life here on earth.

This book is meant to be a road map to inform and instruct you on how live a life so that Jesus one day may tell you, "Well done, good and faithful servant; enter into the joy of your lord" (Matthew 25:23). It provides solid biblical references to those whom Jesus says this, so you can ensure your life will shine as gold at the judgment seat of Christ. It also provides biblical truth so that you will know how you may confidently secure heavenly rewards. It includes practical application on how to live your life to be pleasing to the Lord and helps you place yourself in a position where He might shower you with the rewards promised in Revelation to those who overcome.

Each chapter closes with a story from my own life and a section of application called "What Will You Do to Have Your Best Life in Eternity?" These sections are intended to challenge and encourage you in your walk with Jesus and bring about the "rewardable" increase of sharing the gospel. Don't be discouraged if you struggle at first. If you trip or stumble, as we all do, let Jesus help you back to your feet. The journey is always worth it.

It's not enough simply to assume that you'll hear the words "well done" based on your efforts, motivations, or self-evaluation. Within this book lies the secret on how to *make sure* you will hear Jesus Christ say this most coveted phrase to you.

Because I travel often with a national ministry, I have also included a small section with an analogy of our Christian life to air travel, which I think you will enjoy. Lastly, there are introspective questions to help you apply the material, ensuring your best life forever in heaven!

Chapter 1
A Life That Pleases God

*Only one life, 'twill soon be past,
only what's done for Christ will last!*
—C. T. Studd

Your place in heaven is secure in Jesus Christ. But whether He will say to you "well done" when you arrive there is not guaranteed. Yogi Berra is credited with saying, "It's hard to make predictions, especially predictions about the future." Yet, I predict—even guarantee—that if you intentionally apply the simple truths you will find in the following pages, you will enter into one of the greatest adventures of your life—the type of life that your Master, Jesus, can evaluate as "well done." So let's begin!

Here is something I want you to consider. When you die (which you will 100 percent do), what will you bring with you to heaven? Perhaps you've thought to yourself what you hope heaven might be like. But have you ever considered that you *can* bring something from earth to heaven with you? It's a common misconception that heaven is a place where life takes a pause. While it's true that heaven is a place of rest and peace, we will also work and have

What will follow you into heaven?

responsibilities there. We will experience life to the fullest. Both worship and rest are important to our Christian walk on earth and will certainly continue into eternity. Also, the work we lived out on earth will not be forgotten. We are actually able to bring something from life on earth—our good works! Revelation tells us, in chapters 2 and 3, "I know your works," "do the first works," "as for your works, the last are more than the first," "for I have not found your works perfect before God." In eternity God is very interested in and evaluates our life by our works.

My beautiful wife, Valerie, and I have said regarding heaven, "We will be satisfied just getting in the door!" As believers, we don't need to worry—the good news is that the door is already open to us through the redemptive work of the cross. In Matthew 7, Jesus told us, "Ask, and it will be given to you; seek, and you will find; knock, and it will be opened to you. For everyone who asks receives, and he who seeks finds, and to him who knocks it will be opened" (vv. 7–8). This is a promise you can trust in. But let's not confuse the topic of works as a salvation issue. Your good works do not "earn" you getting into heaven. We know that the only reason we will be in heaven is by the finished work of Jesus Christ: "But this Man, after He had offered one sacrifice for sins forever, sat down at the right hand of God" (Hebrews 10:12).

> Grace will get you into heaven, but your life on earth earns the rewards there!

This "one sacrifice" covers your sins eternally and freely. Paul made this abundantly clear as well when he said, "And if by grace, then it is no longer of works; otherwise grace is no longer grace" (Romans 11:6). You are saved by the grace of God, and that's not your own doing, in case anyone should boast (see Ephesians 2:9). But though grace will get you into heaven, your life on earth earns the rewards there!

Heavenly rewards and those precious words "Well done, good and faithful servant" go hand in hand. Being given eternal rewards is dependent on your life bringing increase with that which the Master has entrusted to you for His kingdom. When you are faithful with your life, when you seek kingdom increase, you live with greater joy on earth and certainly in glory. This kingdom-based joy is natural when you are in a relationship with Jesus. Notice what Jesus had to say regarding faith and works: "Abide in Me, and I in you. As the branch cannot bear fruit of itself, unless it abides in the vine, neither can you, unless you abide in Me" (John 15:4). Jesus used the metaphor of a vine and branches to explain the natural result of a relationship with Him—good works. You are not able to "bear fruit" or good works on your own, but only through intentionally growing your faith. That comes by drawing near to God and being in fellowship in the body of Christ on earth. Faith and works are inseparable and naturally develop together. And the sober reality is that the *quality* of your life in eternity is currently being earned now, by your choices on earth. Right decisions here on earth will bring you extravagant blessings forever!

The fact that some people will have better rewards in heaven, leading to a better experience of life there, is clearly seen in Scripture. Paul wrote that all of our works will either be wood, hay, or straw; gold, silver, or precious stones—(see 1 Corinthians 3:12) and that they will be rewarded accordingly. Certainly being in heaven at all is immeasurably wonderful. But this passage of Scripture reveals there is more. There are clearly degrees of reward that will make our experience in heaven even better. I will explain this concept in great detail in the following chapters.

Few believers consider that the *quality* of life in eternity is earned by our choices on earth. Actually, few believers serve and do good works to obtain rewards. Contrarily, we serve Jesus as an act of sheer gratitude. Yet, bearing fruit is a command, one that will bring joy. The good news is that God has created and destined you for kingdom fruitfulness! In Colossians 1 Paul said that it is his prayer that the believers of Colossae would "walk worthy of the Lord, fully pleasing Him, being fruitful in every good work and increasing in the knowledge of God" (v. 10). This is not just a command for the believers then; it is also an example for us today of what it means to walk with the Lord. To please Him, as you daily walk with Him, you not only will produce good works, but your desire for good works will increase. When your life is fully surrendered to God, you are able to become who you were always purposed by God to be.

You do not belong to yourself but have been bought at a very high cost (see 1 Corinthians 6:19–20). It took the price of God's Son, because your eternal soul, *you*, are precious to Him. You are God's personal possession! He personally paid for you to be His own! While this truth might seem restrictive at first, it actually allows you to live more fully and freely, no longer bound by sin. If you belong to God, He watches over and provides for you. And when you belong to God, you no longer belong to sin or to the world. Titus 2:14 agrees: "[He] gave Himself for us, that He might redeem us from every lawless deed and purify for Himself His own special people, *zealous for good works*" (emphasis mine). What a powerful verse! Not only does it tell of God's "cleanup job" on you, taking you out of rebellion and making you fit for the work by purifying your life, but it also shows that you are His own possession—there's an intimacy here! You can be secure that you belong to the One who created you and knows you fully.

> **You are God's personal possession!**

Think of that for a moment, friend... *You are God's personal possession*, like a fine necklace or prized keepsake! Even if you feel broken, you can rest assured that you have been made whole through Jesus sacrifice on the cross. You are valuable to God and belong to Him alone. What this means is that your life matters very much, that God knows you personally, and that He treasures you deeply!

This verse in Titus also says that as one of His people, not only are you to do good works but you are to be eager and "zealous" to do them. You have been redeemed for a purpose, and that is to do the work of the Lord while you are here on earth. It is not only an obligation but a joy! Again, it's important for you to remember that good works are *not* a salvation matter. You are saved by grace alone, and you can't do anything to earn this privilege (see Ephesians 2:8–9). But still, God highly prizes good works and even expects them of you. We see this reflected throughout the writings of the apostles Paul and James.

When Paul wrote to the church in Corinth, he told them to "be steadfast, immovable, always abounding in the work of the Lord, knowing that your labor is not in vain in the Lord" (1 Corinthians 15:58). God's desire for you and me is a life abounding with good works. There are two important things we should remember.

> **You are to give yourself fully to kingdom work.**

First, God created you for good works. Speaking to the church in Ephesus, Paul proclaimed, "For we are His workmanship, created in Christ Jesus for good works, which God prepared beforehand that we should walk in them" (Ephesians 2:10). God has crafted and shaped you according to His design. You are uniquely and wonderfully made. He has planned good works for you to do, and you are and will be rewarded when you do them!

Second, works quicken your faith. James, in his letter to the twelve tribes of Israel, implored his fellow believers to care for one another. He urged them to love their neighbor and to meet the needs of their community. He tied these actions directly to their faith:

> What does it profit, my brethren, if someone says he has faith but does not have works? Can faith save him? . . . Thus also faith by itself, if it does not have works, is dead. But someone will say, "You have faith, and I have works." Show me your faith without your works, and I will show you my faith by my works (James 2:14, 17–18).

Jesus Chose You for Good Works

Your faith naturally should result in works, according to both Paul and James. You have been redeemed for a purpose; you have an eternal destiny, and your earthly actions matter. In fact, they are rewarded! The value placed on your life producing good works is validated in the words of our Savior: "You did not choose Me, but I chose you and appointed you that you should go and bear fruit, and that your fruit should remain, that whatever you ask the Father in My name He may give you" (John 15:16).

Jesus intentionally created and *chose you*! He wants you to do good works and assures you that the "fruit" you bear in this life will last. When your heart is aligned with God's purpose for your life, you can rest assured that whatever you ask for in Jesus name will be given to you. Jesus wants your life to be rich and meaningful, even here on earth! You can trust the good news that your works have purpose and bring you closer to the God who made you. God is all in regarding you. He believes in you! This is wonderful news . . . and it gets even better! Jesus offers two other insights here:

First, He has *appointed* that your works will be productive in your calling.[1] He has predetermined it to be so. This means that your best efforts will produce lasting eternal impact, not just through your own diligence but through the outworking of God's plan. You already know the outcome!

Second, you have been given much in your earthly life! No matter your financial status, Jesus has in essence given you His credit card to do the work of eternity: "*Whatever* you ask in My name, that I will do, that the Father may be glorified in the Son" (John 14:13, emphasis mine).

God determined (before you were born, in fact) that your life would bring increase, *and* He has committed His resources to you to make it happen. His plan anticipates action and your willing participation in the good things He has in store for you. He has set up—actually in advance—great things to come from you.

> God is all in regarding you. He believes in you.

Jesus told us, "Most assuredly, I say to you, he who believes in Me, the works that I do he will do also; and *greater works than these he will do*, because I go to My Father" (John 14:12, emphasis mine). When you believe in Jesus, your life can be abundant in good works to bring eternal treasure. How would you live your life tomorrow if you knew God was eager to give you everything you need to *win big* for His kingdom?

Second Chronicles 16:9 says, "The eyes of the LORD run to and fro throughout the whole earth, to show Himself strong on behalf of those whose heart is loyal to Him." While this passage is referring to a specific period of time in Israel's history, the qualities of God's character in searching out those who are faithful to Him hold true today. God sees when you honor Him with your actions, and He rewards it. He is waiting to reward loyal hearts. These are marvelous promises from God Himself.

Jesus promised that you would do greater things than even He did! And God's eyes are looking for those who are bold enough—who have a heart—to take Him at His Word. He's looking for those who believe in faith that God can mightily use them on earth!

Is this you? Without faith it's impossible to please God (see Hebrews 11:6), but with faith all things are possible to those of us who believe (see Mark 9:23). You can bring joy to the King of heaven. Isn't that an amazing reality? With these magnificent promises and God's full intent for your life to do great things, you can and should overflow with good works for eternity! You have every reason to steward your life well. The often-neglected reality is that once you arrive in heaven by grace, on that great day, God will be looking for *increase—good works*—from your life. While your sin will no longer remain and you will be able to live in freedom, the results of your earthly actions have an eternal impact. Your heavenly rewards will be based on the works that you have done on earth for His kingdom. In the next few chapters, we will look closely at these rewards.

This principle of God examining your works is reflected in the parable of the vineyard owner, which begins, "When the season came, he sent a servant to the tenants to get from them some of the fruit of the vineyard" (Mark 12:2 ESV). This fascinating story that Jesus told goes on to describe the mistreatment of the master's servant by the tenants when they try to hoard what they have been given. The tenants even go on to murder the vineyard owner's son (vv. 7–8). We can see the spiritual implications here, that God is the owner and lends our lives to us, even sacrificing His own Son, and that Jesus was rejected by those in the world He came to save. You must remember that your life is not your own—you didn't choose to be here, after all. But you were chosen, bought at the price of God's Son. He is in heaven, a far country. When the time comes for His return for you, He will be expecting your life to show faithfulness. You can wait in grateful anticipation of that day!

Great blessing awaits those who follow Christ and live out God's commands. You may have heard the saying "I have never seen a U-Haul behind a hearse." It's true that your material possessions will fade away (see Matthew 6:19). Yet, the startling reality is, you actually can bring something with you from earth to heaven . . . your works!

Frederick Robertson was a fiery English preacher who actually memorized the ENTIRE New Testament in both English and Greek! I love these words where he emphasized our actions:

> **You actually can bring something with you from earth to heaven . . . your works!**

> "Christian life is action: not a speculating, not a debating, but a doing. One thing, and only one in this world, has eternity stamped upon it. Feelings pass; resolves and thoughts pass; opinions change. What you have done lasts—lasts in you. Through ages, through eternity, what you have done for Christ, that, and only that, you are."[2]

Our identity in heaven is being shaped dramatically by our choices on earth today. You have a heavenly assurance of blessing ahead of you when you are faithful! What Robertson said over 150 years ago applies today. His words essentially say that *Christian* is a verb. Or at least, it should be. As we've seen, your faith is confirmed by your actions. You have the power of Christ working within you, and He has a good plan for your life. You can change the world for Jesus—or at least your corner of it!

Still, Robertson's message goes beyond passively following God's will. In the sermon passage above, he implied that what you actually *do* in applying your faith (i.e., your actions) for Christ on earth will *define* your *eternal* existence. Think on his words: "What you have done lasts—lasts in you." This is a bold claim! Is it biblical? Consider this passage: "'Blessed are the dead who die in the Lord from now on.' 'Yes,' says the Spirit, 'that they may rest from their labors, and their *works follow them*'" (Revelation 14:13, emphasis mine).

There is much that is mysterious in the book of Revelation, such as the "voice from heaven" speaking in this verse to whom the Spirit responds. But what is certain is that you have eternal blessing and that your works are directly tied to your rewards. How you spend each day and all that God has given you is an investment strategy that has eternal ramifications at the judgment seat of Christ. This is found in 1 Corinthians 3:14, which says, "If anyone's work which he has built on it endures, he will receive a reward." Your works will last if they are true and tested. In the following chapters, we will look at this passage more fully to examine how God evaluates your works and rewards. But you can be confident that you are building up stores of treasure in heaven!

> **The good news is that your good works do not depend on you, but God!**

If this feels a bit like the pressure is on, that's because there's no avoiding the truth that your actions do carry responsibility. They matter to God. It is a sobering thought that the way I live my life on earth will follow me throughout eternity. Yet the good news is that your works do not depend on you or your effort alone—they are dependent on God working through you. If it were up to us, our good deeds would be like "filthy rags" to Him (Isaiah 64:6). But you are not on your own! You have a helper to come alongside you. Look what the apostle Paul wrote in a section called "Watering, Working, Warning" in the New King James Version:

> Who then is Paul, and who is Apollos, but ministers through whom you believed, as the Lord gave to each one? I planted, Apollos watered, but God gave the increase. So then neither he who plants is anything, nor he who waters, but God who gives the increase. Now he who plants and he who waters are one, and each one will receive his own reward according to his own labor.
> For we are God's fellow workers; you are God's field, you are God's building. (1 Corinthians 3:5–9)

It's a fascinating passage where the apostle Paul wrote about the work he and Apollos had done, presumably in evangelism and disciple-making, in building the church. Paul wrote that good works build on those of others to bring increase ("I planted, Apollos watered"). But we first have to do the work! He went on to stress the importance of building on the foundation God has laid through the cross, as it is the only firm foundation. His words are a warning not to take our faith lightly or become passive. Notice how many verbs appear in these verses: ministers, believed, gave, plants, waters, receive. As Robertson said, living faithfully is "a doing." But even though the "doing" begins with you, it ends with God. Paul wrote that though they were in fact laboring, they were nothing—it is God who brings the increase (v. 6).

At the end of the day, it is God who blesses your efforts (v. 7).

He is the One who grows your small seeds of faith and good deeds. We see this in another parable Jesus told. "[The kingdom of God] is like a mustard seed, which a man took and put in his garden; and it grew and became a large tree, and the birds of the air nested in its branches" (Luke 13:19). God is willing and able to grow your faith into more than you could imagine! We all have purpose in His kingdom. Increase, you see, is the great issue of eternity—the very thing Jesus is looking for to commend you with the words "well done."

> Like a gardener, God is intent on cultivating fruit for His kingdom in you.

We can see in 1 Corinthians 3:9 that Paul used two metaphors to describe who you are in Jesus: a field and a building. A field, or garden, is a magnificent place where human volition and divine providence work together to bring life. Think about it. You could go into a garden with labor, but nothing is going to happen unless God does His part. We see this in Jesus parable of the sower (see Matthew 13:3–9). You can be faithful to sow the seeds of the gospel message to those around you, but God brings the outcome. This, I believe, is how God sees your life and the work He has called you to do. He sees your efforts and rewards them.

It is with mixed feelings that I remember my father and mother sending us into our garden. Two times a week we would trudge out, hoe and rake in hand, maneuvering among the potatoes, tomatoes, and green beans. We would distinguish between what was vegetable and what was weed and carefully remove the weeds from the plants. It required work! Still, we were not alone; we were working alongside our father. He was the one who planted; he was the one who owned the land; and we were out there with the hoes and shovels working for him and with him. (However, unlike the Lord, he never paid us!)

So it is with you. God sends sun and rain in the seasons of your life (yes, He sends the rain too). He may have to "pull weeds" out of your life. God does all of this with a purpose—we are laborers together with Him. His foundation is firm, and we can trust His good work in us to bring abundance.

The nature imagery Paul used to describe the work God does through His people is found in several places in Scripture and certainly was one of Jesus favorite metaphors. Jesus often referred to Israel as an olive tree or as a vineyard that He planted and was preparing, cultivating, and farming. If He did this with Israel as His chosen people, despite their frequent disobedience, how much more us, His very church? As you think on God's care, consider this question: What does the garden of *your* life look like?

> **God may have to "pull weeds" out of your life.**

As Christians, we have been given the undeniably good gift of salvation through Jesus Christ. This grace is unearned and freely received. Still, God expects us to bear the fruit of good works and brings the necessary experiences into our lives to enable this increase—yes, even the difficult ones. When you do bring increase, you are given earthly and eternal rewards. The next chapter reveals the conditions upon which you will receive one of the best rewards: hearing Jesus say, "Well done, good and faithful servant."

Departures			
TIME	TO	GATE	REMARK
10:00	HEAVEN	A10	DELAYED
10:02	HEAVEN	A03	ON-TIME
10:08	HEAVEN	A06	CANCELED
10:09	HEAVEN	A12	ON-TIME
10:12	HEAVEN	B07	ON-TIME
10:14	HEAVEN	B02	DELAYED
10:21	HEAVEN	H07	ON-TIME

Security Check-In

Where do you find your security when the trials of life come? Much like going through security checks before a flight, there are guidelines that God has put in place for your safety, which are found in His Word. They keep you secure in Him and set you up for success. But sometimes turbulence still hits. What do you do then? For me, those times are a reminder to check in with myself to consider where I am finding security in my own life.

In 2016, my team was shepherding an important national ministry, PreBorn! And I was running (too) hard to make it happen. I was functioning largely out of balance, with little margin in my life, finding security through my own efforts. Then God decided to pull some weeds in my garden.

My twenty-eight-year-old daughter, Grace, began to have headaches. This was not completely unexpected, because when she was two years old, she had a brain tumor. The Lord used a local children's hospital to save her life, and over the next twenty-six years she grew into a young woman of inner beauty, purity, and strength. Though the ravages of cancer had left traces of its presence on her outward appearance, she was a loving, joyful, faith-filled person.

But the headaches persisted. They were increasing, and the doctors could not find the cause. Of course, we feared that cancer had come back and checked for it multiple times. It was a dark time of anxiety for all of us. The tests failed to detect the presence of a growing tumor until it got large enough that it was inoperable. In February a CT scan revealed the brain tumor that took her earthly life six months later.

I believe that this dark thread in the tapestry of my life was allowed by God. It was part of the cultivation of the garden of my life, a time to lean into God's firm foundation. I carry the experience as a daily reminder to prize more deeply those around me and to give them the time they deserve. It brought a greater degree of balance into my life.

And God, true to who He is, in this most difficult hour, brought a tremendous blessing. Without my presence in the ministry, it dramatically grew by over 70 percent that year. One thing is evident: I didn't make it grow—God did. My life was realigned, and I saw that the ministry did not depend on my effort, for which I am grateful.

God cultivates, weeds, and waters your life that you might fruitfully and productively work with Him to glorify

Him. He grows your character through trials and hardship, building up your faith. It is important for you to remain in Him, even during the difficulties of this life, as the day will come when the fruit of your labor will be rewarded—or not—by the Lord. Now let's look together at this day of personal evaluation and rewards—heaven's "test day"—in the next chapter. It will be a day of celebration!

What Will You Do to Have Your Best Life in Eternity?

This chapter discusses two important concepts in your Christian walk. The first is that you not only are willing to do good works for God's kingdom, but that you are zealous and eager to do them. The second is that your life is carefully cultivated, like a garden, to bear more fruit. Here are some questions to consider:

1. Jesus said in Matthew 7 that a tree will be known by the fruit it bears. What kind of fruit is your life bearing?

    Good fruit: love, joy, peace, longsuffering, kindness, goodness, gentleness, meekness, faithfulness, self-control (see Galatians 5:22-23)

    Bad fruit: selfishness, anger, adultery, rebellion, idolatry, hatred, envy, murders, drunkenness[3]

2. What are some practical steps you can take to "amp up" the fruitfulness of your life? Consider how you are stewarding your time, talent, and treasure.

3. What is your reaction to the truth that God seeks to greatly use your life for His glory? How then should you live? What would you do for God if you knew you could not fail?

4. Have you ever considered the idea that your earthly life will impact your experience in heaven?

5. In what ways might God be growing your character through a present trial? What are some ways you can lean into the community of believers to help you through this time?

Chapter 2
Well Done, Good and Faithful Servant!

*It ain't what you don't know that gets you into trouble,
it is what you know for sure that just ain't so.*

—Unknown

I was recently on an airplane traveling from Dallas to Houston. The man beside me was reading a book on theology and the media, so I naturally assumed he was a Christian. When I asked him about his faith, he told me that he was not only a believer but a Dallas Theological Seminary tenured professor. So I asked him, "On that great day, what would you want to hear when you arrive in heaven?" Predictably, he told me, "I'd want to hear 'well done, good and faithful servant.'" But to my surprise, when I asked him who, biblically, will hear "well done," he hesitated, staring at me, then out the window in thought. The question stretched into a long silence. He did not know the answer.

So don't be concerned if you can't answer it either. That, friend, is why I've written this book! After all, it's not about what you *hope* will bring those precious words—it's about what the Bible, the Word of God, says. What does the Bible have to say about *who* Jesus will commend? If you hope that He will say these words to you, it is important to understand *why* He said them—the biblical context, if you will, of His compliment "well done." I want to share what Scripture says is Jesus intent for your life on earth and how He desires to accomplish that purpose through you. I've discussed how God is the One who brings the increase, and in the following chapters I'll examine precisely and biblically who Jesus will say "well done" to—and how that can be you!

I am sure you desire and believe that your "forever life" in heaven will be better than you could possibly imagine. I certainly do. But what if many of the things you think you know about heaven are biblically inaccurate?[1] Often, our beliefs come from shows, movies, culture, or even what other Christians tell us, rather than from the source: God's Word. If you've struggled to understand what heaven will be like, you are not alone. Hearing "well done" is one of the most important aspects of our Christian faith, yet I have found, through many conversations, that only one person in about a thousand actually knows what the Bible says about eternity.

You may have heard this question: "If you were arrested for being a Christian, would there be enough evidence to convict you?" If a jury were to examine how you spend your time and money, would it greatly differ from your unchurched neighbors or coworkers? I like the way Greg Laurie put it: "You must turn from the power of Satan to God. A lot of people today want to live in two worlds. If you want to be a Christian on Sunday, but want to live the other way the rest of the week, it won't work (2 Corinthians 6:14)."[2] When you have the joy of salvation in Jesus Christ, then it is your joy to live a life that is dedicated to Him in all that you do.

Maybe, like the rich young ruler in Mark 10, you feel confident that you are honoring God's ways. Perhaps you, too, are able to say to Jesus, "Teacher, all these [commands] I have kept from my youth" (v. 20). Surely, if your enthusiasm, time, and passion for Jesus are a significant part of your life, you will hear those most desired words when you get to heaven—"Well done, good and faithful servant."

At first, this appears to be a reasonable belief. However, we dare not risk *assuming* Jesus will tell us, "Well done." Let's take a look at Jesus response to the young man: "Then Jesus, looking at him, loved him, and said to him, 'One thing you lack: Go your way, sell whatever you have and give to the poor, and you will have treasure in heaven; and come, take up the cross, and follow Me'" (v. 21). In this case, generosity, a focus on others, and dying to selfish desires were all necessary to be rewarded in heaven. It is the same today. Whether we take the young man's words as truthful or a bit embellished, we can see in Jesus loving but truthful response that something more than best efforts, love, and zeal for the Lord must be present to serve Him well. But what does this look like in everyday life?

> **We dare not risk assuming Jesus will tell us, "Well done."**

When I think of someone who is an example of this kind of life, Claire, my delightful sister in Christ, comes to mind. Claire was interviewing for a position as a counselor in our ministry. I already knew that she was a faithful Christian. But as we were conversing during her interview, what displayed her true passion for Jesus was her response when I asked her a fairly standard question: "What is it you like to do in your spare time?" There are an endless number of surface-level activities she could have shared, but she didn't hesitate. Her reply was joyful and immediate. She told me, "I enjoy going down to the Santa Monica Pier with my mom and sharing the gospel with those who are passing by."

I instantly hired her! Here was evidence that her love for

Jesus reaches beyond Sunday morning church attendance, important as that is. Her faith influences every aspect of her life. She cares enough about her relationship with Christ to use her spare time to tell others about Him in one of the most liberal, cosmopolitan areas of the country! Certainly a court could easily convict her of being all about Jesus.

Friend, this action-focused Christianity holds one of the most treasured secrets of the faith. Like Claire, you can discover this hidden joy. It is key to the one thing you as a believer hope to hear Jesus Christ say to you when your time on earth is complete. Let's look at the biblical context for hearing those precious words.

> To whom will God say the most coveted words in creation: "Well done, good and faithful servant"?

One of the most blessed sentences in all of God's Word is found in the book of Matthew: "His lord said to him, 'Well done, good and faithful servant; you have been faithful over a few things, I will make you ruler over many things. Enter into the joy of your lord'" (25:23). To whom will God say the most coveted words in creation: "Well done, good and faithful servant"? This statement comes from the lips of Jesus Himself in Matthew 25:14–30 within the parable of the talents. It is a familiar story:

> For the kingdom of heaven is like a man traveling to a far country, who called his own servants and delivered his goods to them. And to one he gave five talents, to another two, and to another one, to each according to his own ability; and immediately he went on a journey. Then he who had received the five talents went and traded

with them, and made another five talents. And likewise he who had received two gained two more also. But he who had received one went and dug in the ground, and hid his lord's money. After a long time the lord of those servants came and settled accounts with them.

So he who had received five talents came and brought five other talents, saying, "Lord, you delivered to me five talents; look, I have gained five more talents besides them." His lord said to him, "Well done, good and faithful servant; you were faithful over a few things, I will make you ruler over many things. Enter into the joy of your lord." He also who had received two talents came and said, "Lord, you delivered to me two talents; look, I have gained two more talents besides them." His lord said to him, "Well done, good and faithful servant; you have been faithful over a few things, I will make you ruler over many things. Enter into the joy of your lord."

Then he who had received the one talent came and said, "Lord, I knew you to be a hard man, reaping where you have not sown, and gathering where you have not scattered seed. And I was afraid, and went and hid your talent in the ground. Look, there you have what is yours."

But his lord answered and said to him, "You wicked and lazy servant, you knew that I reap where I have not sown, and gather where I have not scattered seed. So you ought to have deposited my money with the bankers, and at my coming I would have received back my own with interest. So take the talent from him, and give it to him who has ten talents.

"For to everyone who has, more will be given, and he will have abundance; but from him who does not have, even what he has will be taken away. And cast the unprofitable servant into the outer darkness. There will be weeping and gnashing of teeth."

While you may have heard this story before, have you applied it to your own life? Do you know what it means for you? Before we dive deeper into the literary conventions Jesus used and the historical background, here is a summary of the main events of the parable. The man (who is, as we will later see, an example of Jesus) was about to go on a journey and gave three of his trusted servants (that's us, believers) possessions of his talents in different amounts: to one he gave five, another two, and another a single talent.

Notice how he gave a different number of talents to each of them. While the account does not describe in detail why he made this decision, we can logically conclude that he gave to each according to their ability. Here is the biblical principle of responsibility—he didn't favor one more than another, despite what we may initially think. There is no mention of an initial judgment and no indication that he thought any less of the servants who received fewer.

> God gives us talents according to what we can handle.

Instead, he gave them each what they could handle. They each received what they needed.

In the same way, God gives you only that which you are able to handle through trusting in Him. Likewise, He won't allow us to be overcome by more than we can handle (see 1 Corinthians 10:13). On our own we are weak, but in Him we are strong (see 2 Corinthians 12:10). We are each given unique trials and blessings, valleys and mountains. But the good news is that we are never alone. God delights in walking beside us and providing us with seasons of blessing. While we all are made in *Imago Dei* (God's image), we have been created as individuals with distinct gifts. Some of us may be artists, while others are scientists, builders, doctors, or theologians. No matter your gifting, God says you are beautifully and wonderfully made (see Psalm 139:14). If you were not given the skill set of a great orator, you are not expected to be Billy Graham, but you are still meant to use your giftings faithfully, just as Billy Graham was expected to use his oratory skills for the gospel. As Bruce Wilkinson said, "Whatever our gifts, education, or vocation might be, our calling is to do God's work on earth."[3]

God expects you to use your life's abilities, possessions, influence—your "talents"—to bring increase with your life. It is your destiny to increase the kingdom and receive God's blessing in return. What is this blessing? Wilkinson described this well in *The Prayer of Jabez*: "To bless in the biblical sense means to ask for or to impart supernatural favor. When we ask for God's blessing, we're not asking for more of what we could get for ourselves. We're crying out for the wonderful, unlimited goodness that only God has the power to know about or give to us."[4] God wants to share His good gifts with you, just as the master in Jesus parable did with his servants!

In the context of this parable, Jesus described the servants' faithfulness as being measured by the actions they took to *increase* the portion they were given (in this case financially). By way of application, it is evident that God defines faithfulness not by a strict list of dos and don'ts, but rather by our efforts to *bring increase* for His kingdom. This extends beyond tithing and church attendance into every

> **God doesn't define faithfulness as dos and don'ts.**

aspect of our lives. Christianity is not a religion that looks inward but instead a relationship that reaches out to others. God wants you to use the blessings you have been given to faithfully serve Him, which can only be done by sharing these blessings (the best of which is salvation) with others.

This desire for increase is innately built into everything God does. From the very beginning it was the first commandment God gave to man: "God blessed them, and God said to them, 'Be fruitful and multiply; fill the earth and subdue it; have dominion.'" (Genesis 1:28). There are interesting implications here for how human beings are meant to relate to and interact with the natural world, but for our purposes we will focus on what this verse means for how we are to relate to one another. Like with the trees and all of creation, God was looking for increase within human relationships when He said, "Be fruitful and multiply." While God does bless new life through procreation, His command here also sets a pattern for how you are to live in the world He created—you are intended to treat increase as a way of life. Increase and growth are naturally built into everything God does. From the beginning of creation until today, God has ordained that if something is not growing, it is in decline and will eventually die, just as you will if you are cut off from Him (see John 15). The necessary conclusion is that God desires fruitfulness from you. We see this principle at work not only in the natural world but also in both the Old and New Testaments, as examined above. God's Word, His nature, and His desires for you do not change. He laid out a pattern you can continue to follow today.

> **Increase and growth are naturally built into everything God does.**

What the master gave to his servants in the parable of the talents was a true treasure. It was more than just a symbol of trust and loyalty. The master was after more than monetary increase; it was a test of their love for him and their overall stewardship. It is easy as a modern reader to skim over the details since we may be unfamiliar with many of the cultural practices and systems that provide the background for Jesus parables. But if we take the time to dig a little deeper, in this case examining the currency of the time period, we'll gain further insights.

Historically, one denarius was the usual payment for a day's labor, and a talent was roughly the value of twenty years of work by an ordinary person. One talent is worth roughly $1,500,000 in today's U.S. currency—a vast sum of money![5] I believe Jesus used the example of this large amount to make a point. The point is that God has given you and me a true treasure: the gift of our earthly life *and* eternal life through His Son. He used an extreme amount of money in the parable (a lifetime's worth of money) to help us realize He seeks a lifetime of stewardship with *all* He has entrusted into our lives. Just as the master returned and asked for an accounting from his servants, Jesus is coming back to reward us and see what we have done with our life—and with this most precious possession, our salvation. Bringing increase to the Lord through your life of increase for Him will give God, as the Master in this parable, great joy in heaven, just as the parable says: "Enter into the joy of your master."

The First and Second Servants

When the master returned to inspect his investment and called his servants into account, here's what he found: two of his servants, the one who had five and the one who had two talents, each had *doubled* the talents that were entrusted to them—they brought *increase*. By bringing increase, they honored him. These servants were the ones to whom the master in the story offered those precious words: "Well done, good and faithful servant; you have been faithful over a few things, I will make you ruler over many things. Enter into the joy of your lord" (Matthew 25:23). Their actions gave their master great joy that he wanted them to enter into! So, too, your earthly life can produce heavenly joy!

The key lies in faithfulness with what your Master (Jesus) entrusts to you. But what does faithfulness look like?

> Your earthly life can produce heavenly joy!

Interestingly, the servant who was given two talents was not expected to earn the same amount as the one who was given five. When the master returned, he did not compare their earnings. If he had, the second servant would have come up short. Instead, he looked at the portion that was given and the effort put into increasing it to determine faithfulness. Both the one who was given five and the one who was given two helped increase what he entrusted to them. Both were told, "Well done." You can do the same for the kingdom.

Jesus (the master in this parable) is seeking more than mere financial faithfulness from us, His servants. He is seeking a lifetime (thus the lifetime value of the talents) invested in bringing Him increase. The talent is a symbol of the fullness of all we are from His generous hand.

God has given you unique abilities, skills, resources, and the precious treasure of the gospel of Jesus Christ, and He desires you to use it to make disciples—to increase. Heaven is a place of unending joy, and there is rejoicing in heaven over every sinner (we all fall into that category, by the way) who comes to know Him. Luke 15:10 tells us, "Likewise, I say to you, there is joy in the presence of the angels of God over one sinner who repents." Every individual matters to God, so they should matter to us as well. We have been sent into the world to make disciples and to increase God's heavenly kingdom. This is both a privilege and a responsibility. The reality is that God will hold us accountable for the increase our life brings. Jesus is coming back—sooner than any of us know—to inspect what we have done with what He entrusted to us. This is a reason to rejoice and gives us purpose for eternity!

Ask yourself, *What talents has the Lord given me? Am I using them faithfully? Is my life bringing increase?* Scripture shows that on that great day when we stand before Him, increase will be one of the metrics—a yardstick—by which we will hear those words we long for.

Finally, we have a clue as to what Jesus may have been alluding to in this parable of the talents, when He said, "Enter into the joy of your lord." First of all, how do we know that the lord (or "master," in some translations) in Jesus story refers to our Lord? To make this connection, it is helpful to examine the Greek word used here: *kurios*.[6] While there are a number of different words that Jesus could have used,[7] He used a term that conveys both humanity and divinity. This term can be interpreted to mean "lord," but it has other uses as well. Jesus was called *kurios* by the woman at the well before she knew His divine identity, as well as Paul describing Him as the Son of God.[8] This unique meaning is particularly suited to this parable, as Jesus was treating the master as both a human figure and as representative of our Lord. Knowing this, we can take the phrase "enter into the joy" as a promise from God to us. This is good news!

> **Joy is the serious business of heaven.**

On that day in heaven when God says to you, "Enter into the joy of your master," you will find that it has been your earthly privilege, by your faithful works, to bring joy to God Himself! He will be joyful because of how you lived your life, and He will, on that wonderful day, invite you to enter into His joy, to share it with you. It is both a command and a delight for you to live out in your Christian walk. This theme of rejoicing is found elsewhere in Scripture—even in Jesus own words, as we saw in Luke 15.

To live a life that brings heavenly reward, we must make it our mission to be alert to opportunities that can bring joy to God. We can play a significant part in causing rejoicing in heaven by leading one sinner to repentance. In other words, successful witnessing is where the Holy Spirit and the Word of God convict a sinner to repent. This requires effort and may not always be easy, but it will be worth it.

The Third Servant's Accounting

Let's return to Jesus parable, and look at the remaining servant. The third servant in the parable of the talents did not bring increase—and his lack of increase displeased the master. In fact, the master said, "Cast the unprofitable servant into the outer darkness. There will be weeping and gnashing of teeth" (Matthew 25:30). This language is reminiscent of the language describing hell. While this idea may be sobering, you must take seriously what God takes seriously. At the same time, you do not have to live in fear once you have given your life to Christ. Your salvation does not depend on your good works, and God does not send born-again believers to hell for not bringing increase. So there must be a bit more to this third servant.

It becomes quickly clear, when we examine the story more carefully, that this servant did not know his master, as the servant begrudgingly describes him as harsh and cruel. He excuses his lazy behavior by saying, "I knew you to be a hard man, reaping where you have not sown, and gathering where you have not scattered seed. And I was afraid" (vv. 24–25). The third servant deflects his own guilt by casting blame onto the master and calling into question his character. He goes on to confess that he buried the talent. This is the point where the master calls him "wicked and lazy" (v. 26). The reason he is called lazy is because he did not extend the effort to trade the master's talent as the other servants did. He didn't even put the money in the bank, where the master would have received the most basic increase of interest on it.

Still, we might argue that this doesn't seem fair. I mean, the third servant was not particularly *un*faithful—after all, he didn't *lose* the master's talent. He protected it, kept it safe . . . but did not increase it—not at all. As a result, he received a scathing rebuke from the master. Why? It is apparent here that it is not enough to just get by with doing the bare minimum. God's Word describes this as being as useless as hiding your light under a basket (see Matthew 5:15). Jesus is serious about your life bringing increase. This is your destiny as a follower of Him! This increase is the condition upon which you will hear "well done." And if you do not bring increase, it is a very displeasing matter to your heavenly Master. Friend, this doesn't need to be your story. Are you bringing increase with your life?

I am concerned that many believers today are very much like this third servant. They know the treasure of God's Word, revere it, study it, highlight it in yellow, memorize it, hide it in their heart. And all of these actions are good. But they do not *use* it to bring more souls, more increase, to the Master and His kingdom. They play it safe. This is not enough to earn heavenly treasure. Playing it safe with God will not be rewarded.

> **Playing it safe with God will not be rewarded.**

We see this principle borne out in a similar parable in Luke 19, the parable of the minas—the only other place where we see the commendation "well done." To summarize, it says,

> Now as they heard these things, He spoke another parable, because He was near Jerusalem and because they thought the kingdom of God would appear immediately. Therefore He said: "A certain nobleman went into a far country to receive for himself a kingdom and to return. So he called ten of his servants, delivered to them ten minas, and said to them, 'Do business till I come.'" (vv. 11–13)

Since the same Greek term *kurios* is used throughout this parable, we can conclude that the nobleman here, too, is another representation of Jesus in both His humanity and His divinity, similar to the master in the parable of the talents. From there, it is not much of a leap to discern what sort of a "kingdom" this nobleman might be seeking. This parable is arguably an analogy of Jesus ascension into heaven to receive His heavenly kingdom (a far country). We also see here that the nobleman entrusted ten of his servants with his treasure—minas—in this parable, one each. Now look carefully at the next phase—"Occupy till I come" (Luke 19:13 KJV). The word *occupy* here means to do business, trade with it, earn more, invest—bring increase, bear fruit.

Here again we see an accountability with three of the ten servants. The first one to recount his earnings had one mina and returned ten more. The nobleman said to him, "Well done, good servant; because you were faithful in a very little, have authority over ten cities" (Luke 19:17). A reward! And the second came saying, "Master, your mina has earned five minas"

(v. 18). The nobleman commended him also and rewarded him again with cities—five of them! Both servants were rewarded in an abundant fashion—in some aspects, far greater than the extent to which they increased the nobleman's assets. We see the generosity of God toward faithfulness to lavish blessings on you when you bring increase! In fact, the nobleman called their faithfulness to what they were given a very small matter. He rewarded the first and the second servants with the leadership of an entire city for each mina that they stewarded to increase. Although minas in that day were worth less than talents (a talent was worth nine years of work),[9] ten minas were still a decent sum—about a quarter of a year's wages (or one hundred days) for an agricultural worker. Though the nobleman called it a small matter, he esteemed the value of it by rewarding a city according to each mina increased.

In terms of heavenly rewards, it is not immediately evident what this means when the nobleman said, "Have authority over ten cities" (v. 17). What are the cities and how were they to take charge? The Bible gives us some clues in other parts of Scripture to help us further understand this, and we can trust that it will be an exciting prospect: "And he that overcometh, and keepeth my works unto the end, *to him will I give power over the nations: and he shall rule them with a rod of iron; as the vessels of a potter shall they be broken to shivers*: even as I received of my Father" (Revelation 2:26–27 KJV, emphasis mine).

We will examine more comprehensively our rewards, how God evaluates our life, and what His reward system is in heaven in chapter 5. For now, we can observe that the servant was rewarded with a promise of what he would receive in heaven. Suffice it to say, we have plenty to look forward to, beyond what we can even imagine! But that isn't the end of the story.

Faithfulness Requires Action

There is a common technique in storytelling called the "rule of three" that Jesus used effectively in many of His parables. So it shouldn't surprise us that we are introduced to a third servant in the parable of the minas, just as in the parable of the talents. Let's look at the third servant's actions: "Then another came, saying, 'Master, here is your mina, which I have kept put away in a handkerchief. For I feared you, because you are an austere man. You collect what you did not deposit, and reap what you did not sow'" (Luke 19:20–21).

Based on the pattern we saw in the parable of the talents, we can probably guess what comes next. The third servant had disobeyed—he did not follow instructions to bring increase. What sort of accounting did he get? The nobleman quickly removed the servant's original mina and gave it to one who was the most faithful! Because he did not increase what he was given, he had to give up everything he had. As with the first parable, it hardly seems fair, until we consider that faithfulness requires action. And so, we see a second example of an accounting that expects us to increase what the master entrusts us with if we hope to hear the words "well done." We also see that a reward follows for those who do. In the same way, we are eligible to receive rewards when we are faithful.

Like the two servants in the parables who did not bring increase, there are eternal consequences if we do not bear fruit, use the gifts God has given us, and share the gospel. The two slothful servants provide a welcome warning that we may avoid facing the judgment of not bringing increase if we consider how we steward our life on earth. The flip side is that, like the servants who did bring increase, we, too, will be given abundant blessings when we are good stewards. The differentiation of the rewards we will receive in heaven, as earned by our earthly works, are shown in detail in the next chapter, whether they are gold, silver, and precious stones or wood, hay, and stubble. We earn heavenly rewards (not salvation) while on earth.

This lesson is contrary to natural inclinations. But it is good to be warned that if we play it safe like the servant with one talent or one mina did, then when Christ comes back, we will be stripped of our heavenly rewards. But there is good news too! If we wisely are faithful with what God has given us, we will shine as stars in eternity.

> 'Those who are wise shall shine like the brightness of the firmament . . . like the stars forever and ever' (Daniel 12:3).

As Christ's church, His bride, we are to be people of action—*church* is a verb. *Christian* is too!

◆ ◆ ◆

You can earn God's pleasure and reward in heaven by faithfully using your talents here on earth: "But be doers of the word, and not hearers only, deceiving yourselves" (James 1:22).

How do these parables affect your preconception of hearing the words "well done" when you meet the Master? Many believe that they will hear those words predicated on their devotion and effort and sacrifice. But Scripture reveals the real reason is by bringing increase for eternity with our lives. If we do, our rewards will be magnificent on that day we stand before Him. I encourage you

> **We earn our heavenly rewards (not salvation) while on earth.**

to strive to be a ten-talent person on that great day by bringing much increase for the Master. In the next chapter we will take a closer look at that great and awesome day before the Lord.

TIME	TO	GATE	REMARK
10:00	HEAVEN	A10	DELAYED
10:02	HEAVEN	A03	ON-TIME
10:08	HEAVEN	A06	CANCELED
10:09	HEAVEN	A12	ON-TIME
10:12	HEAVEN	B07	ON-TIME
10:14	HEAVEN	B02	DELAYED
10:21	HEAVEN	H07	ON-TIME

Book Your Ticket

With the ministry, I travel all the time. What was once viewed as an impossibility a century ago (the miracle of flight) is now an ordinary part of my reality. I've encountered many types of people who have many different beliefs. Throughout this book, I will share some of their stories with you. But first, I will share one of my own. To travel anywhere, you first have to know where you are going and then choose and commit to your destination. So, I ask you, What are you waiting for? Let's dive into this journey of hearing "well done." Here is the first story in our flight together.

When I was ten years old, my parents thought it was a good idea to enroll me in swimming lessons. Perhaps they were right, but that didn't matter to me. I distinctly remember the bus pulling up to the curb. As I shuffled in, head down, I glanced at the other children, looking for a sign that anyone else was nervous too. None of them seemed as concerned as I was. They jostled one another, eager to get where they were going. They talked to their friends. They laughed. That bus was full of joyful noise with kids ready to leap into the local pool. Problem was, I wasn't one of them. I was deathly afraid of water. I didn't want to dive into the deep end or even splash in the shallows. It didn't matter whether I had a new swimsuit or whether the other kids were having fun without me. At the pool, I held on to the railing with white knuckles for as long as I could, until the swimming instructor finally, after what felt like hours, coaxed me to give it a try. I didn't want to be floating and free; I wanted to feel secure.

Fast-forward five years, and my parents bought a small lake-based campground in the Midwest. You might think that young boy from swim class gripping the railing would stay far away from the lake, but since then, I'd overcome my childhood fear. It no longer gripped me the way that it used to. Thanks to my parents' insistence, even in the face of my pleading, I'd graduated from swim class and was no longer afraid to dive into the deep end.

And this campground was a young man's dream! Canoes, woodlands, wildlife, and—significant in my mind at the time—girls. The campground had a beach, and my parents needed a lifeguard. Because they had subjected me to the swimming lessons as a child, I was able to train and become the leader and lifeguard there. Giving me a position among my peers was a bit of a windfall as a young man running that beach. How the tables had turned! What once was a place of dread had become a place of privilege, teaching me responsibility and discipline.

What are you afraid of? What might God do with your life if you let go of fear and live faithfully in His freedom? With your life on earth, you have been given a one-way ticket to your eternal destination. What are you doing now to prepare for the journey of a lifetime?

What Will You Do to Have Your Best Life in Eternity?

Your salvation is the greatest entrustment, the most precious treasure of your life. It gives you hope beyond the grave and the promise of eternal life. Are you increasing your talent or keeping it to yourself? Here are some questions to consider:

1. What talents has God given you? In what ways are you using them for His glory?

2. Why do you think the third servant chose not to invest the master's money? What are some of the things that hold you back in living for Jesus?

3. If bringing increase to God's kingdom is the measurement of hearing the words "well done," what is one step you can take this week to further His kingdom? How can you encourage others in their faith?

4. How does the concept of you bringing joy to the God of heaven and earth make you feel? How does it impact the way you relate to those around you?

5. What is one fear holding you back? What is one action you can take to combat that fear? How will you hold yourself accountable?

Chapter 3
Your Personal Day Before God

He is no fool who gives what he cannot keep
to gain what he cannot lose.
—Jim Elliot

I can sincerely say that I've never met anyone who doesn't like going to the beach. Sun, sand, a breeze on your face, water lapping at your feet. What could be better than a relaxing day oceanside? There are people on the shore building sandcastles, sand tunnels, sand caves . . . I've seen it all! And they'll actually spend entire days doing it—hours upon hours. Some people even go pro building things out of sand, entering competitions and winning prize money. But whether it's a three-story castle made by a professional sand sculptor or a lopsided pile patted into shape by a toddler, everybody knows the inevitable will happen. The rushing tide will come in, and their entire work will be leveled. The sand will be returned to the ocean. It will be trampled underfoot and forgotten.

In that way, we certainly don't want this to be the picture of our life's work when it's evaluated in heaven! We want it to be lasting, pleasing to the Lord, and rewarding to ourselves. When the tide comes in, we want what we've built with our life to stand on a firm foundation. This chapter is about how to build our life on the only enduring foundation.

God is cultivating your life here on earth. Whenever you face trials, it is your comfort to know that the fruit you produce through your endurance is building your faith and will be rewarded in eternity. Your hardship produces blessing! It will not be wasted. This gives meaning to your struggles and difficulties in this life, as you remember there is another life to come where you will no longer face persecution or pain.

So how do you know whether you will have your best life in eternity? There is but one heaven, God's dwelling place and our ultimate home. This place of eternal joy awaits all those who put their faith in Messiah Jesus. Yet some will enjoy greater rewards than others. In this chapter, we'll explore how our works on earth will be tested—and rewarded—by God in heaven. We will take a look at the refining fire of God that reveals good works. Let's begin by examining how we can know whether our works will last.

It's important to clarify here that while this chapter focuses on whether our works will be gold, silver, and precious stones or wood, hay, and stubble, the greatest reward is that we'll be in heaven by the works of Jesus, not our own. Every tear will be wiped from our eyes, and we will be living in the presence of God in eternal joy! However, heaven's rewards are predicated on our works and will impact the rewards we will enjoy in heaven forever. The reward of your works will make your experience in heaven unique.

> **Everyone's experience in heaven will be unique to them.**

First, we must turn to God's Word to understand what sort of works the Christian life should produce. Think about where you find meaning, particularly during times of hardship. Are you able to hold on to your faith and remember that your works will be rewarded? What works do you find cropping up in your life? Do you see the fruit of the Spirit in your actions toward others?[1] You don't have to guess what good works God cares about. He has already given us a guide! Scripture defines for us what God truly values about our life's work—that solid foundation upon which we *must* build our lives. Paul explained this in his letter to the church at Corinth:

> According to the grace of God which was given to me, as a wise master builder I have laid the foundation, and another builds on it. But let each one take heed how he builds on it. For no other foundation can anyone lay than that which is laid, which is *Jesus Christ* (1 Corinthians 3:10–11, emphasis mine).

What Paul was saying here is that we labor, but it's only by God's grace that we even have the privilege of working together with Him. You have been *chosen* by God to help build His kingdom! This is good news. God doesn't need your works to complete His purposes, but He chooses to work with and through you anyway! You can

> **Our works should be a stage upon which Jesus Christ is displayed.**

trust that He has a masterful design for your life. This is where you can find joy and meaning, even when circumstances are not going your way. God is building up the church and His kingdom, and you will live with Him forever, being blessed by the good works that you have done for Him on earth. Paul went on to caution the believers regarding how they labor: "take heed." They were not to build through their own strength for their own purposes, but instead to rely on what had already been laid for them. This is a directive to us as well. We must be careful about how we do our labor—our work *must* be built on the first, preeminent thing: the foundation, Jesus Christ!

Here we find a challenge to us as believers today. We may do many charitable works—feed the hungry, provide access to clean water, build homes, donate our clothing. These many wonderful works of compassion are the essence of doing God's work. In fact, when we do these acts, we are doing them for the King (see Matthew 25:35–40). We are being the hands and feet of Jesus when we bring the good news to those we are serving. But the "good" is often different from the "best."

If the truth about Jesus gets excluded or neglected in doing these good acts of compassion, we are missing the whole point. Even nonbelievers are able and willing to do good deeds. If we do the many good deeds a hurting world so desperately needs and yet leave the truth about Jesus out of it, we might as well be an earthly ministry instead of the church of Jesus. While anyone can offer food, water, shelter, or clothing, it is Jesus alone who offers eternal life—something beyond material comfort. Our good works are best validated if they are done for the purpose of bringing people to know Jesus. Our works are to be a foundation for telling people about Jesus Christ's salvation.

> Our life's work for God should point to eternity.

The foundation and purpose for all of Christian action is the gospel. In other words, if you're going to build for God's kingdom, the first thing is this: it has to be *about Jesus*! Your good works will only last and have eternal value if they are done for Him. God cares about the motive of your heart and whether you are sharing His good news with a hurting world. There are many good deeds for which the world may commend you. But if you do these charitable works and neglect the gospel, then you're not truly caring for your neighbor. Paul's words in 1 Corinthians said that if you build your foundation on the work of Jesus Christ, your reward in eternity will be great! God wants to shower blessings on you.

This vital principle is modeled best in the very person of our Messiah. Throughout Jesus divine life He consistently fed, healed, and ministered to the physical needs of people. Yet He did not stop with that nor consider those actions of compassion to be an end in themselves. For instance, let's examine Jesus interaction with a woman from Samaria:

> A woman of Samaria came to draw water. Jesus said to her, "Give Me a drink." For His disciples had gone away into the city to buy food. Then the woman of Samaria said to Him, "How is it that You, being a Jew, ask a drink from me, a Samaritan woman?" For Jews have no dealings with Samaritans. Jesus answered and said to her, "If you knew the gift of God, and who it is who says to you, 'Give Me a drink,' you would have asked Him, and He would have given you living water." The woman said to Him, "Sir, You have nothing to draw with, and the well is deep. Where then do You get that living water?" (John 4:7–11)

Jesus began by acknowledging a physical need: water. But He used this need as a starting point to share with the Samaritan woman how she could receive "living water" through Him—salvation. Instead of focusing purely on meeting the physical needs

> **Jesus used compassion as a platform to transform the hearts of people.**

of those around Him, Jesus used these important occasions as a segue to address their greater need—how to enter into the kingdom of heaven, of which He is King! Jesus used compassion as a platform to transform the hearts of people. He used the drawing, universal appeal of meeting physical needs as a validation and inroad to the hearts of men and women—and so can you! Friend, the message you have is one that others need to hear. You have the wonderful chance to bring them good news.

Ultimately, the first principle we see in the example of the woman at the well is that works must find their purpose in Jesus Christ. You must live focused on the saving grace that is found only in Him; that is, good works produced by faith.

True Gold Fears No Flame

If you've ever sat around a bonfire at dusk, telling stories, roasting marshmallows, and watching the flames turn logs to ashes, then you've seen that different materials burn at different rates. While pine cones spark and pop, logs slowly wear down to embers over time, providing a cozy glow.

But fire can be destructive too. I visited my friend in Southern California after the devastating fires there in 2018. Every home on the opposite side of his street was completely destroyed. Only the concrete foundations of the houses and some charred studs remained. While wood may leave a remnant of existence, grass and hay leave none. In the same way, your good works are made of different materials and will be tested by fire to see which are lasting and which will fade away.

The following verses provide a picture of how God will evaluate your life's work in heaven. Notice, He does not tell us that we will be rewarded by the extent of our effort. It will not be by the sacrifices we make, not by our sincerity or great intentions, however wonderful they may be. If we do things in the name of love or in the name of compassion yet neglect Jesus, we've missed the mark entirely. Our works will be judged (and rewarded!) by whether or not they are founded, grounded, and purposed *on Jesus Christ.*

Let's look again at 1 Corinthians 3: "Now if anyone builds on this foundation with gold, silver, precious stones, wood, hay, straw, each one's work will become clear; for the Day will declare it, because it will be revealed by fire; and the fire will test each one's work, of what sort it is" (vv. 12–13).

In these verses, we can see that our works are not all of the same quality or mettle. Some are stronger and more precious, and others are weaker and more common. Further, we know that

> **Will anything remain of your earthly works after the testing fire of God?**

the true worth of our works will be revealed. Our works will be tested, the passage tells us, by fire. The whole of your life's work will be exposed to the testing fire of God. What will endure this fire? "If anyone's work which he has built on it endures, he will receive a reward. If anyone's work is burned, he will suffer loss; but he himself will be saved, yet so as through fire" (vv. 14–15).

This is fascinating Scripture! We've already seen that there will be a day in which our works done on earth shall be declared and revealed in heaven. We know that even if the works burn up, we have been saved to eternal life through Jesus sacrifice if we accept it. He has already walked through fire for us. Still, we can eagerly anticipate heavenly rewards when we build on His foundation. This is a day that we can look forward to if we are living by faith and putting our trust in Jesus!

The location in heaven where this testing will occur is called the Judgment Seat of Christ. Speaking to the believers in Corinth, the apostle Paul talked about being present with the Lord and the judgment seat of Christ:

> We are confident, I say, and willing rather to be absent from the body, and to be present with the Lord. Wherefore we labour, that, whether present or absent, we may be accepted of him. For we must all appear before the judgment seat of Christ; that every one may receive the things done in his body, according to that he hath done, whether it be good or bad. (2 Corinthians 5:8–10 KJV)

This is the place of evaluation of the *works* of the believer, not of his or her salvation. The unsaved, those who did not come under the lordship of Christ, will not appear here at all. They will appear before the great white throne judgment of God. Theirs is a place of condemnation, whereas ours is a place of great reward. "Judgment" here does not refer to accusation, disapproval, or blame, but rather to a process where our works are sifted and merited rewards are given. Your eternal destiny includes blessings and heavenly responsibilities! So this is the trial for the works of believers—it is the *bema* (Greek for "judgment") seat of Christ![2] This is a joyful time, which every believer can eagerly anticipate.

> **The judgment seat is about evaluation of works and rewards, not condemnation.**

Let's use our sanctified imagination for a moment. You are at the judgment seat of Christ in heaven. There appearing is every Jesus-following human being who ever lived on earth for all time—*billions* of people, standing in the presence of God. People crowd one another, masses tightly packed as far as the eye can see. It is a jostling, noisy bunch, and you can't so much as hear yourself think. And then, all of a sudden, the moment is here. A hush falls over the crowd. It's strange to have such complete silence with so many people surrounding you, but everyone is straining to see their Lord. Even though there are billions present, you know that your moment is coming. And then you see Him, the Ancient of Days, in white clothing:

> The hair of His head was like pure wool. His throne was a fiery flame, its wheels a burning fire; a fiery stream issued and came forth from before Him. A thousand thousands ministered to Him; ten thousand times ten thousand stood before Him. The court was seated, and the books were opened. (Daniel 7:9–10)

The opening of the books signals the distributing of heavenly rewards. One by one, we each get our moment to step up on the altar before the Lord—and there, for *all* to see, are the works of your life, what you have done. Charities, mercies, days of devotion, serving, teaching, giving, study, prayer, worship to God—what you have done with the talents you have been given on earth—it's all there. Not only that, but everyone is watching, waiting for their own turn. According to Romans 14, "We shall all stand before the judgment seat of Christ. . . . So then each of us shall give account of himself to God" (vv. 10, 12). It is a moment of celebration, where you will be rewarded for the good deeds you did on earth, even those you did when you thought that no one was watching!

> **"Our God is a consuming fire."**

Then in a breathtaking moment, like Elijah facing down false prophets at the altar soaked with water (see 1 Kings 18:20–40), the presence of the living God descends upon your works. Your life works are tested by holy fire!

What is this fire? Well, we know that fire in Scripture often reveals the presence of God. For instance, He appeared in a burning bush to Moses (see Exodus 3:2) and a pillar of fire to the Israelites, guiding them out of Egypt into the wilderness (see Exodus 13:21). When Elijah mocked the priests of Baal and challenged them to a showdown, the fire of God burned up Elijah's sacrifice and licked up the water on his altar. In the New Testament, on the day of Pentecost, God sent the Holy Spirit with tongues of flame (see Acts 2:3), and Revelation says that our Lord Jesus eyes are like flames of fire (see 19:12)! Our response can only be that we "serve God acceptably with reverence and godly fear. For our God is a consuming fire" (Hebrews 12:28–29).

Scripture shows that the presence of the Holy God is the fire that will test the works of your life to see whether they are wood, hay, stubble, gold, silver, or precious stones. (Remember 1 Corinthians 3—it will all be "revealed by fire.") His presence is enough to reveal and make plain the true desires and motives behind your outward actions. Your earthly works should be—and will be—tested by *this one thing*: Is Jesus Christ present and part of your works . . . or not? God will evaluate if and how fully your works are glorifying Jesus and pointing to His redemptive work on the cross. This should be motivation to consider how your works glorify Jesus Christ and His gospel—His very purpose in coming to earth.

In one of many interactions, the people following Him asked Jesus directly about the works of God. "They said to Him, 'What shall we do, that we may work the works of God?' Jesus answered and said to them, 'This is the work of God, that you believe in Him whom He sent'" (John 6:28–29). I am glad Jesus made it so plain and simple! Your works *have to be* about Him.

How much of Jesus Christ is in the works of your life? Friend, as long as you are sharing the gospel message and living your life for Him, you can be certain that your works will matter in heaven! After testing your works' relevance to Jesus, then their quality, sacrificial nature, and level of success can be evaluated.

We've already seen that God differentiates between the *quality* of each person's work. Second Corinthians 5:10 says, "We must all appear before the judgment seat of Christ, that each one may receive the things done in the body, according to what he has done, whether good or bad." We know that sinful works have been judged at Calvary, so this is not about condemnation since that judgment fell on Jesus; this is about whether your works are everyday earthly works or eternally relevant.

> **How much of Jesus Christ is in the works of your life?**

"Christian" works in our fallen race and world are performed with many differing motivations and intentions. Some are for God's glory alone. Some are for funds, for pity, for pride, and for a host of other desires. Not all seemingly good works will last. But we know with certainty that the basis for the evaluation of all works on that great day in heaven—the foundation, according to the Bible—is Christ. The good news is that it won't be a surprise; this is a truth from Scripture that you can rely on!

Your life and works can only become holy as they are purified and infused with Jesus Christ. All refining processes require pressure and heat. Mike Goeke, a pastor who uniquely served both in San Francisco and now Midland, Texas (two diametrically opposed cities), explained, "To refine gold, heat must be applied to force the impurities [dross] to the surface. As the impurities rise, they are removed and more heat is applied. This process continues and continues, heat is applied and re-applied, until the gold is pure. The refiner knows the gold is pure when he looks into the gold and *sees his clear reflection*" (emphasis mine).[3] When God examines—gazes into—your life, He wants to see the reflection of Jesus in you.

> God loves you too much to leave you as you are.

You may hope for a quick remedy in God's refining of the impurities in your life. The pressures and struggles you face can be difficult to bear. Yet an immediate fix is not the nature of the refining process—not for gold, and not for you. God loves you too much to leave you as you are, because your impure self cannot reflect all of who He is. He loves you too much to give you an easy but impermanent solution. Instead, His change is lasting and fully transformative. Your fullest joy is realized in the growing brilliance of the reflection of Him in your life. Only then can you become who God always intended you to be.

The concept of God refining your faith and character as gold is refined can be found throughout Scripture. Peter wrote about this process:

> In this you greatly rejoice, though now for a little while, if need be, you have been grieved by various trials, that the genuineness of your faith, being much more precious than gold that perishes, though it is tested by fire, may be found to praise, honor, and glory at the revelation of Jesus Christ. (1 Peter 1:6–7)

We know that our trials have eternal purpose and meaning, that we will ultimately have joy and blessing!

Through these passages, we have seen that there is a refining process on earth and testing again by fire in heaven. We know that how we get to that defining moment (heaven and the judgment seat of Christ) in the first place is by faith alone in Jesus Christ and that the only thing that can last in the fire of God is our works that glorify Jesus. This is our motivation on earth to consider what foundation our works rest upon. Yet a question remains: What will be the results of this testing by fire? When the dross has been removed from the gold, and the wood and hay separated from the precious stones, what happens next?

For the answer, let's return to 1 Corinthians 3. In verse 14, we see that after the testing of God's holy fire, there is the concept of reward: "If anyone's work which he has built on it endures, he will receive a reward." Now, I don't know about you, but the very fact that I get to be in heaven, avoiding hell and enjoying the gift of eternal life is plenty! What more could a person want? And yet there *is* more! There are *rewards* in heaven. Theologians can only conjecture what these rewards look like. But considering that God can do *anything*, it is obvious the rewards there are going to be magnificent beyond our comprehension—rewards distributed to those of us whose works endure. In the next chapter we will look closely at the specific rewards described in the book of Revelation that are awaiting those who bring increase with their lives.

> **God's rewards will last millions of years in a timeless eternity.**

In verse 15 we are reminded that this is not an issue of salvation but rather an issue of gain or loss in heaven: "If anyone's work is burned, he will suffer loss; but he himself will be saved, yet so as through fire." You can be confident from this that there is both *gain* and *loss* awaiting you there, but your salvation is secure! You have everything to gain. The only thing you have the prospect of losing is the rewards that God wants you to earn in your life. Jesus Himself said in Matthew 10:42, "Whoever gives one of these little ones only a cup of cold water in the name of a disciple, assuredly, I say to you, he shall by no means lose his reward." We see here that if, in your compassionate works, you are discipling people for Christ, there are indeed rewards laid up for you in heaven.

So this judgment seat of Christ is nothing to fear, but instead holds the wonderful prospect of providing you with a better heavenly life. The rewards that you are given and experience there will last forever—millions of years on the first day in a timeless eternity. This, then, makes your works and existence on earth a proving ground, a training camp, a construction project, which will have a lasting impact on your quality of life *forever*! One of my favorite verses is found in Revelation. It speaks directly to this concept and is often my daily prayer: "And behold, I am coming quickly, and My reward is with Me, to give to every one according to his work" (22:12).

This is my great desire, that He would perfect in me His work and that I would not be just acceptable but instead very satisfying to Him when He's done with me. James 1:4 says, "But let patience have its perfect work, that you may be perfect and complete, lacking nothing."

The word *perfect* here in the original language means "complete, whole" rather than "flawless." Truly, God has set before us an investment plan for blessing. The plan is that the more directly your life efforts are founded on Jesus Christ, the better quality your eternal life will be! This is exactly why Paul said our life works must first be built on the foundation of Jesus: "For no other foundation can anyone lay than that which is laid, which is Jesus Christ" (1 Corinthians 3:11). You don't have to reach a state of perfection to be eternally rewarded, just purpose your efforts to point to Him. As stated in chapter 1, "Blessed are the dead who die in the Lord from now on . . . and their works follow them" (Revelation 14:13).

◆ ◆ ◆

The truth is, you and I will live to see all that is written in this chapter *in person*—you will be there! It is your forever destiny. So, what are you setting yourself up for in eternity? What will your life in heaven consist of . . . and what does the Bible say about the nature of God's blessings? In the next chapter, we will explore these heavenly rewards further. We will examine in exciting detail the things God has waiting for those to whom He says, "Well done!"

Departures

TIME	TO	GATE	REMARK
10:00	HEAVEN	A10	DELAYED
10:02	HEAVEN	A03	ON-TIME
10:08	HEAVEN	A06	CANCELED
10:09	HEAVEN	A12	ON-TIME
10:12	HEAVEN	B07	ON-TIME
10:14	HEAVEN	B02	DELAYED
10:21	HEAVEN	H07	ON-TIME

Standby

When flying standby, you have to be prepared to board the plane at a moment's notice. Whether you've been delayed, had your flight canceled, or need an earlier flight than you anticipated, you might be able to get a seat—if you're lucky and ready at the gate when they call your name. In the same way, you don't know when Jesus will return, so you must be ready at all times. You are to wait eagerly for Him and do good works that glorify His name. But unlike flights that get delayed, Jesus has perfect timing. Unlike planes that get overbooked, Jesus has already prepared a place for you in heaven. You don't need to worry that you will miss out on eternity, as long as you live for Him.

I remember one time when I was unexpectedly forced to wait for my flight. I was laid over on a late flight in Dallas . . . four hours due to "inclement weather," as they say. While I have great respect for the pilots and airline workers who make these judgment calls about when it is safe to fly, in the moment it seems like an inconvenience to travelers like me who just want to get wherever it is we're going. Sometimes it's easy to be impatient or frustrated by these situations. I'll admit, I was tired, hungry, and out of sorts. This delay was not part of my plan! But it was part of God's plan.

I happened to have a free pass to the airline club, so I decided to go there to work and rest. *At least it will be quieter,* I thought. As I sat down in the secluded back area of the room, I wasn't planning to start a conversation. But I noticed a Jewish man sitting nearby who was wearing a yarmulke. Suddenly, I felt the tug of the Holy Spirit prompting me to go up to him. Now, he did not have a robe or the Hasidic garb, so I was fairly certain he was not Hasidic, but I thought I would get his attention. I greeted him and then asked, "Are you a Hasidic Jew?"

He immediately replied, "No, but I am a conservative Jew, and I believe the Bible is true from cover to cover!"

Well, this was a clear opening for a fun conversation indeed! The verse that immediately came to my mind was Isaiah 53:5, which says, "But He was wounded for our transgressions, He was bruised for our iniquities; the chastisement for our peace was upon Him, and by His stripes we are healed."

I replied, "That's great, I, too, believe the Bible is the inspired, inerrant Word of God. So, what do you believe about Isaiah 53?" And I quoted the verse.

"I believe it speaks of the Messiah," he said.

"I do too!" I replied. "Do you know that Jesus Christ fulfilled this perfectly, as well as over seven hundred other Old Testament prophecies?"

What he said next revealed that he was struggling with this in his life. He said, "I don't believe this—you sound just like my mother. She is always talking to me about Jesus and has brought up that verse. She is involved with Jews for Jesus in Jerusalem. She often speaks with David Brickner, the executive director!"

I could see this was an area where God was pursuing him and working on his heart. We had a vibrant conversation about many other messianic and even prolife passages that deeply challenged this Jewish man and demonstrated that while he said he believed the Bible was true, he actually was deeply conflicted in some of these areas.

God met him personally that evening, and I got to be a part of it! It certainly was not convenient being delayed for four hours. I wouldn't have chosen to wait in the airport rather than board my flight. But had I not been alert to what God was up to in the delay, I would have missed a rare opportunity to speak with a Jerusalem Jewish businessman and witness God convicting his heart. I have a suspicion that God purposefully delayed me to give me the opportunity to reach this man with the truth of the Messiah and to challenge my own faith in the process. God's plan is trustworthy, and His timing never fails.

What Will You Do to Have Your Best Life in Eternity?

1. Do you know anyone whose life could be characterized as zealous for good works? What are their attributes?

2. In your weekly choices, how does your faith in Jesus rank (in how you spend your time, talent, and treasure) as opposed to entertainment, sports, hobbies, family, and work? Brainstorm ways you can prioritize Him in your daily life.

3. Examine your service for the kingdom. Does it intentionally lift high the name of Jesus Christ and His finished work on the cross? Is it relevant to eternity?

4. What do you think distinguishes a person's life as being gold versus wood or hay?

5. Are you willing for God to interrupt your busy routine to take the time to share your faith with another?

Chapter 4
Your Rewards in Heaven

That day, which you fear as being the end of all things, is the birthday of your eternity.

—Seneca the Younger

Have you ever won a raffle, door prize, or participation trophy? As exciting as it is to win, these are prizes that you haven't earned. You get them if the luck of the draw is in your favor, or if you attend the event or play in the game just for showing up. On the other hand, academic scholarships, sports recognition, and promotions are awards merited by your achievements, hard work, or diligence. They are intended to measure your performance and the efforts you've put into practice. Receiving earned rewards is gratifying indeed. But even these rewards have limitations. Students, athletes, and coworkers may cheat to get ahead or be praised for natural talent despite a lack of effort. It can be disheartening to work hard yet not see your efforts pay off. Thankfully, that's not how it is in God's kingdom!

In the preceding chapter we examined how living your life intentionally to glorify Jesus the Son of God means that you will shine like gold, silver, or precious stones at the judgment seat of Christ, which is a place of reward rather than condemnation.

We looked at the refining process, which occurs both on earth and in heaven. The refining of your life is tantamount to Jesus final message to you: that you are to share the good news and, by doing so, bring glory to Him. This is the secret to having the assurance that you will hear God tell you, "Well done, good and faithful servant." Using your talents for kingdom purposes is not just an obligation but an opportunity for eternal reward and blessing. This is good news . . . and yet, there's *more* good news!

Not only will Jesus tell you, "Well done," and your works of love be on display—literally on fire for Him—but Scripture also gives a glimpse of the unique and wonderful rewards awaiting you in eternity as a result of a life lived for Christ. As we've seen in previous chapters, beyond the gift of eternal life, you may be given responsibilities, gifts, and authority based on your earthly good works. These rewards are specifically described in God's Word. Through Scripture, we gain a miraculous glimpse into this future heavenly reality.

I am sure you would agree that you do not strive to live a faithful, overcoming life simply to receive rewards. This is not your primary motivation to live for Jesus. It also bears repeating that you do not *earn y*our salvation through your good works. Rather, you pursue holy living because you love Jesus and owe Him everything for what He has given you—His everything on the cross. The garden of your life should produce the fruit of good works out of your abundance of gratitude and joy. Your works should grow naturally when you consider the grace that you've been given. You know that you don't perform good deeds for the sake of blessing alone. Yet God has given knowledge of the results of your works—heaven's rewards—which are recorded in the Bible for your awareness and understanding. Friend, these Scripture passages are a source of hope and joy when you face the difficulties and hardships of this life. They remind you that this is not your home! You have a future promise: an abundant life waits for you.

This hope of heaven and its eternal blessings has, across centuries, motivated Christians to endure persecution and even death because of the hope of this better life. "But now they desire a better, that is, a heavenly country" (Hebrews 11:16). In this chapter, we will closely examine the set of epic rewards awaiting us as we bring fruitful increase with our lives. God is so very good! These rewards awaiting us in heaven are blessings beyond the gifts we've *already* received: redemption, sanctification, salvation. Let me first clarify, however, that heaven's greatest reward is the presence and company of Jesus Christ and His Father. All of your relational desires to know and be known will be fulfilled in eternal companionship with our Lord. "For now we see in a mirror, dimly, but then face to face. Now I know in part, but then I shall know just as I also am known" (1 Corinthians 13:12). Jesus presence is heaven's greatest reward for sure! There will be no more separation or sorrow, but only joy. The apostle Paul understood this: "To me, to live is Christ, and to die is gain. . . . I am hard-pressed between the two, having a desire to depart and be with Christ, which is far better" (Philippians 1:21, 23). While you are on earth, you are to share the good news of the gospel and build relationships with others, but when brokenness enters in, you can trust that God has something better in store. Jesus has already prepared a place in heaven just for you:

> **Heaven's greatest reward is the presence and company of Christ.**

> Let not your heart be troubled; you believe in God, believe also in Me. In My Father's house are many

mansions; if it were not so, I would have told you. I go to prepare a place for you. And if I go and prepare a place for you, I will come again and receive you to Myself; that where I am, there you may be also. (John 14:1–3)

So then, heaven's greatest reward and promise is to be in the company of Jesus Himself . . . to be *where He is*. Nothing will compare to this. Yet, in keeping with the unbounded love of God, His Word reveals there are even more magnificent rewards given to the faithful believer. While being with the Lord Jesus personally is awesome, Scripture addresses more promises for our eternity! Why would we be told about these rewards if we weren't supposed to look forward to receiving them? And how can we better understand the nature of these rewards and ways to prepare our earthly life for eternity?

This, my friend, is sanctified, wise, self-advised living. It is nothing short of an eternal investment plan. Jesus talked of it specifically like that. He advised us to lay up treasures in heaven. These treasures are in fact what God has planned to give to those who have ordered their lives in such a way as to be eligible for these magnificent rewards:

Do not lay up for yourselves treasures on earth, where moth and rust destroy and where thieves break in and steal; but lay up for yourselves treasures in heaven, where neither moth nor rust destroys and where thieves do not break in and steal. (Matthew 6:19–20)

For more proof of God's intent to reward you, let's return to Jesus parable of the minas from chapter 2. If you recall, the servants who were faithful to increase the minas that they were given were told, "Well done," by the nobleman. But not only did they hear "well done," they also were *tangibly rewarded* with authority over multiple cities (see Luke 19:17–19). Since this parable is a depiction of Jesus Christ Himself, we know that He will be returning . . . and bringing blessings!

Like the nobleman in the parable, Jesus went to heaven to receive a kingdom: "But this Man, after He had offered one sacrifice for sins forever, sat down at the right hand of God" (Hebrews 10:12). His kingdom is everlasting, and He is preparing a place for *you* before He returns. This is good news! Jesus is coming back, and He is bringing rewards with Him! Acts 1:11 tells us that "this same Jesus, who was taken up from you into heaven, will so come in like manner as you saw Him go into heaven." Jesus is returning—this is a promise that you can trust in! Although you don't know the hour of His return (see Matthew 24:36), you know that He is bringing rewards for His servants (us) when He comes. Second Timothy 4:7–8 says, "I have fought the good fight, I have finished the race, I have kept the faith. Finally, there is laid up for me the crown of righteousness, which the Lord, the righteous Judge, will give to me on that Day, and not to me only but also to all who have loved His appearing." Along with Revelation 22:12, which says, "Behold, I am coming quickly, and My reward is with Me, to give to every one according to his work," the following Scripture passage confirms that we will be rewarded based on our earthly service:

> **Jesus is coming back, and He is bringing rewards with Him.**

> The nations were angry, and Your wrath has come, and the time of the dead, that they should be judged, and that You should reward Your servants the prophets and the saints, and those who fear Your name, small and

great, and should destroy those who destroy the earth. (Revelation 11:18)

We often think of saints as those who have been canonized in the church, but the term *saint* is used differently in this context.[1] Those who put their trust for eternity in Jesus Christ are referred to as saints throughout the New Testament—that includes you! You don't have to be persecuted or martyred to earn this distinction; you've already been "set apart" by God. Even if you don't feel like a saint, the book of Revelation assures us that those who "fear [God's] name" shall receive rewards!

> **God promises an escalating set of wonderful rewards awaiting you in heaven.**

In studying God's Word, we have found that the hope of hearing the words "well done, good and faithful servant" is inextricably tied to the *increase* we bring with that which the Lord has entrusted to us. The differentiation in the parable of the minas, as compared to the parable of the talents, is the addition of the *rewards* given to those who brought increase. In the parable of the talents, the master commended his servants with "well done, good and faithful servant . . . enter into the joy of your lord" (Matthew 25:23). What was that joy?

Well, we can see many parallels in these two parables, and certainly part of the joy the servants experienced in the parable of the minas was receiving extravagant rewards. It is logical to consider that part of this joy could be blessing and reward in the parable of the talents as well. Although the nobleman described the act of increasing the minas as a small thing, he still gave something incredible to those who were faithful—

just consider the *scale* of the reward he gave (see Luke 19)! To each of the servants who brought increase, he gave authority over entire *cities*! God promises an escalating set of wonderful rewards awaiting us in heaven. Here we get a glimpse that there will be concrete and tangible rewards given to the faithful. How does this correspond to what Scripture says will happen to you in eternity? The concept that you will rule over populations (cities) is actually found in God's Word.

Look at this reference to Abraham: "By faith he dwelt in the land of promise as in a foreign country, dwelling in tents with Isaac and Jacob, the heirs with him of the same promise; for he waited for the city which has foundations, whose builder and maker is God" (Hebrews 11:9–10). God is building a city for you to dwell in! This is a promise of blessing that He has given to all believers. Knowing this, Abraham was content not to have a permanent dwelling place on earth, though he was extremely wealthy. He spent his whole life wandering as a nomad in tents, because he believed the promise he'd been given and chose to hold his earthly life loosely. Abraham knew that God would give him a city in glory! You have that same promise through Jesus Christ. It is your destiny to live with angels in the heavenly Jerusalem with those who have trusted in Him!

> But you have come to Mount Zion and to the city of the living God, the heavenly Jerusalem, to an innumerable company of angels. (Hebrews 12:22)

> I heard a loud voice from heaven saying, "Behold, the tabernacle of God is with men, and He will dwell with them, and they shall be His people. God Himself will be with them and be their God. (Revelation 21:3)

God's rewards are extravagant, as an expression of His character. Paul understood this extravagant nature of God when he said, "Now to Him who is able to do exceedingly *abundantly* above all that we ask or think" (Ephesians 3:20, emphasis mine).

> **God's rewards are extravagant, as an expression of His character.**

The servants in the parable of the minas experienced this as well. They had brought increase with the resource they'd been given and probably knew the nobleman would be pleased. But I am sure they were surprised and likely never expected to be given authority over multiple cities as a reward! In the same way, your heavenly blessings will far exceed all that you can imagine.

As we've seen through Jesus parables of the talents and the minas, beyond the *unearned grace* that got you into heaven, your *efforts* directly impact the quantity of the rewards given by the Master. Both parables show that the master (Jesus Christ) gives rewards *in proportion to the increase you bring*, above and on top of hearing "well done, good and faithful servant." Not only are you given blessings on top of salvation, but you have the potential to earn even greater rewards or responsibilities based on the works you've accomplished during your earthly life. You will be forever grateful that you did! This concept of rewards based on your works is reinforced throughout the New Testament. Now let's turn to Scripture to take a look at the escalating set of promises and the rewards you will receive once you are in this heavenly city.

You will live with God Himself in the holy city on a new earth.

Aside from eternal life in the presence of Jesus, of course, this is perhaps the most exciting reward that you will receive. One day, sin and sorrow will be wiped away, and you will live with God Himself on a new and redeemed earth:

> Now I saw a new heaven and a new earth, for the first heaven and the first earth had passed away. Also there was no more sea. Then I, John, saw the holy city, New Jerusalem, coming down out of heaven from God, prepared as a bride adorned for her husband. And I heard a loud voice from heaven saying, "Behold, the tabernacle of God is with men, and He will dwell with them, and they shall be His people. God Himself will be with them and be their God." (Revelation 21:1–3)

This has the exciting ambience of a wedding ceremony! We as the church of believers are the ones preparing to meet our bridegroom, Jesus. We are adorned not with material items but with the lasting ornaments of good works performed in His name. Friend, He has prepared a place for you to live for eternity. He has been thinking of you before you were born! In this passage, which is a future promise, we find the fulfillment of what every human heart longs for: heaven on earth! There really will be heaven on earth—a permanent home of hope and belonging, blessing and abundance—and you will

> **There really will be heaven on earth—and you will live there!**

live there! Your destiny is to live with God as His own citizens on a newly re-created earth, which will last forever.

You will be in paradise and eat from the tree of life.

This reward is specifically given to those who overcome. (This vital concept of overcoming is one we will look at more closely in chapter 5.) The promise is described in the following passage: "He who has an ear, let him hear what the Spirit says to the churches. To him who overcomes I will give to eat from the tree of life, which is in the midst of the Paradise of God" (Revelation 2:7).

In the garden, man was forbidden to eat of the tree of life and evicted from paradise to keep him from partaking of the tree of life in his fallen state. In Jesus this is restored! Just as man's history began with being forbidden to eat of the tree of life, man's history will consummate in God inviting us to eat of it! We will be welcomed with open arms, as the father welcomed his prodigal son. Remember Jesus promise to the repentant thief: "And Jesus said to him, 'Assuredly, I say to you, today you will be with Me in Paradise'" (Luke 23:43). You have been given the same promise.

You will not be hurt by the second death.

We are given a second promise through the Spirit in the same Revelation passage: "He who overcomes shall not be hurt by the second death" (2:11). Everyone dies once. However, those apart from Christ will suffer a conscious, eternal second death.[2] Much can be said about this; however, the important fact is that if you overcome, you are spared from this. You will never be separated from eternal life with the Lord.

You will have divine sustenance, a privilege, and an intimate name from God.

Not only will you be a citizen of a holy city who may eat from the tree of life and remain unharmed by the second death, but you will also be given three additional rewards when you overcome: "To him who overcomes I will give some of the hidden manna to eat. And I will give him a white stone, and on the stone a new name written which no one knows except him who receives it" (Revelation 2:17). This passage is mysterious but good! Let's examine these rewards more closely.

1. You will partake of spiritual food.

You may remember manna from the story of the Israelites wandering in the wilderness, complaining of hunger and begging God for food to eat. They were sent a miracle—bread from heaven, enough for that day alone.[3] Just as the Israelites received what they needed physically, so, too, will you receive what you need spiritually. The first of the three additional rewards will be "hidden manna to eat" (Revelation 2:17). This will be the fulfillment of what Jesus promised in John 6:35: "I am the bread of life. He who comes to Me shall never hunger, and he who believes in Me shall never thirst." You will have all that you need in Him.

Jesus is the sustenance of the resurrected believer in glory—that's you! You will have contentment and joy in Him. Revelation 7:17 tells us that "the Lamb who is in the midst of the throne will shepherd them and lead them to living fountains of water. And God will wipe away every tear from their eyes." You will be guided and taken care of in eternal life. This "hidden manna" issues from Jesus Himself, which means that you have no need to worry further about your most basic needs. Wonderfully, this blessing even includes addressing the griefs of your heart and making you whole ("wipe away every tear")!

2. You will receive a white stone.

Your second additional reward requires some historical context to fully appreciate what you've been given. The concept of a stone in Jesus time was a voice, a vote, access—a privilege. It was a Roman custom to give white stones with names on them to victors of a contest.[4] In Scripture, we see that God commanded the Israelites, when they crossed the Jordan River, to set up whitewashed stones: "When you have crossed over the Jordan, that on Mount Ebal you shall set up these stones, which I command you today, and you shall whitewash them with lime" (Deuteronomy 27:4).

For the Israelites, this was a monument of victory. It was a commemoration of how far God had brought them and the trials He had already delivered them from. Here is what the Lord commanded Moses to tell them once they set up these stones: "Take heed and listen, O Israel: This day you have become the people of the LORD your God" (v. 9). The Jordan River is often characterized as a passage through death to life, from bondage to freedom, from promise to fulfillment. As the whitewashed monument at the Jordan was a tribute to God's faithfulness, so this heavenly reward of a white stone is a tangible trophy declaring your victory and that you belong to the Lord our God. This is a celebration of Christ's victory in your life!

3. You will receive a new name.

Your third reward for overcoming is that you will be given a "new name" (Revelation 2:17). From the passage, we can surmise that you cannot know what this new name is until you get to heaven and receive the white stone. The word *new*—in the Greek *kainos*—does not mean new as compared to the old in time, but new in the sense of quality.[5] For most of us, our parents or another loved one gave us our names. In a similar way, God, our Creator and Father, will give you a new, truer name, reflecting His special love for and adoption of every true child of His.

This new name carries with it a special intimacy between you and Jesus. The passage tells us that only the two of you will know the name you've been given. This is a bit reminiscent of the intimacy between a husband and a wife. There are things I call my wife that I call no one else—because she is (as you will be with Jesus) my bride. What a wonderful gift to be named and known by your beloved Lord!

You will be given authority.

Along with being named and known by God, you are entrusted with influence. Several passages in Scripture curiously reveal the delegation of authority and power to God's people in eternity. The theme that authority and responsibility will be given to you in eternity is throughout both the Old and New Testaments. While we don't know exactly what this will look like, we do know that God is preparing us to reign and rule in marvelous ways as revealed in the passages that follow.

The apostle Paul encouraged believers to exercise authority in the church in preparation for exercising authority in heaven. The authority that you will be given to reign and judge is expansive. You will be a delegate to have judicial power over both the world and angels.

> Dare any of you, having a matter against another, go to law before the unrighteous, and not before the saints? Do you not know that the saints will judge the world? And if the world will be judged by you, are you unworthy to judge the smallest matters? Do you not know that we shall judge angels? How much more, things that pertain to this life? (1 Corinthians 6:1–3)

The Bible tells us that angels are involved with earthly activity. This concept is found in Hebrews 1:14, for example, which describes "ministering spirits" that are sent to serve believers. While the scope of our authority to "judge angels" is unclear, this passage reveals a responsibility—a blessed reward—that believers will possess in eternity.

Your authority as a follower of Jesus is foretold in the Old Testament through a vision Daniel had of earthly kingdoms rising and falling. In the vision, he was also told about a lasting kingdom: "Then the kingdom and dominion, and the greatness of the kingdoms under the whole heaven, shall be given to the people, the saints of the Most High. His kingdom is an everlasting kingdom, and all dominions shall serve and obey Him" (Daniel 7:27). It is exciting to think that we will be delegated authority in heaven! Although the extent is a mystery, this next promise found in Revelation gives a few more specifics of the exercise of this authority for those who overcome.

You will be given rule and power over nations.

We know from the previous passage in Daniel that Christ will rule over all people groups, nations, and languages ("dominions") in His millennial kingdom. But God includes you too. You are given this promise: "And he who overcomes, and keeps My works until the end, to him I will give power over the nations" (Revelation 2:26). This verse seems to show that you will have some part in this authority. This is good news to all believers!

You will enjoy heavenly clothes, assurance of eternal life, and a personal introduction.

Friend, God wants to bless you into eternity. He is willing and more than able to do so! Since God gives abundant blessings beyond what you could imagine or hope for, there are more rewards to come. Let's move on to the next chapter in Revelation: "He who overcomes shall be clothed in white garments, and I will not blot out his name from the Book of Life; but I will confess his name before My Father and before His angels" (3:5).

As we examine this verse, we notice several things:

1. You will be clothed in white garments.

White clothing is the apparel of the believer in heaven. The color symbolizes Jesus purification of you in His kingdom. You have been made "white as snow" (Isaiah 1:18) through His sacrifice, and in eternity you will be without sin or blemish. You are refined, given sight, and unified with others:

> I counsel you to buy from Me gold refined in the fire, that you may be rich; and white garments, that you may be clothed, that the shame of your nakedness may not be revealed; and anoint your eyes with eye salve, that you may see. (Revelation 3:18)

> I looked, and behold, a great multitude which no one could number, of all nations, tribes, peoples, and tongues, standing before the throne and before the Lamb, clothed with white robes, with palm branches in their hands. (Revelation 7:9)

The white garments referenced here are the sanctified, blood-washed deeds of the saints—those of us who follow Jesus and do His good works.[6] In heaven, you will be made holy!

2. You will have your name in the Book of Life.

That your life, through faith in Christ, has been found worthy is wonderful news! Your name, if you are a believer, will be inscribed in the record-keeping book of heaven,[7] the greatest honor anyone could ask for. This record is called the Book of Life, or the Lamb's Book of Life, and is mentioned in the New Testament. Paul wrote in Philippians 4:3, "I urge you also, true companion, help these women who labored with me in the gospel, with Clement also, and the rest of my fellow workers, whose names are in the Book of Life." We see the Book of Life mentioned throughout Revelation as well: "I saw the dead, small and great, standing before God, and books were opened. And another book was opened, which is the Book of Life. And the dead were judged according to their works, by the things which were written in the books" (20:12).

This promise is perhaps one of the most precious rewards in that it delivers you from eternal separation from your Lord. This Book of Life is none other than the Lamb's Book of Life, and He is the One who decides whose name abides in it: "I will not blot out his name" (3:5). You will be in God's presence for eternity!

3. You will experience Jesus confessing your name before the Father.

Use your sanctified imagination for a moment. You have just entered heaven. Jesus embraces you, and He takes you personally by the hand and says, "I want to introduce you to somebody." He brings you before a 1,500-mile-high throne upon which is seated the Father. Then, with all the angels watching, He says something like this: "Abba, allow Me the honor of introducing My servant, [your name], who just arrived in heaven. You've known her even before her earthly life, and now she is finally home!" This is the reward you will be given based on Revelation 3:5—having your name confessed before the God of heaven and earth and all of the angels surrounding His throne.

You will be a permanent fixture in God's temple, with God and Jesus name written upon you.

A personal introduction to the One who created you isn't the last reward listed in Revelation 3. Verse 12 promises yet another reward. Jesus told us, "I will make him a pillar in the temple of My God, and he shall go out no more. I will write on him the name of My God and the name of the city of My God, the New

Jerusalem, which comes down out of heaven from My God. And I will write on him My new name."

This image of a pillar seems to indicate that Jesus will assign, to the one who overcomes, a firm and abiding place in the everlasting kingdom of God. This concept also appears in Galatians 2:9, where Peter and John are referred to as pillars by virtue of their strength of character. In heaven you will have a place of permanence, which you will never have to leave.

Furthermore, Jesus will indelibly identify you with the New Jerusalem, Himself, and His Father—He will write these three names on you. This is a mystery for sure, although the Scripture becomes clearer when you consider what significance names have today. You experience this naming in a lesser fashion in your own life. For example, when you travel to a different land, someone may ask your identity by your family name and the place from which you come (your citizenship). Similarly, you will be marked and identified as belonging to God and a permanent part of the New Jerusalem—your new home!

You will be seated with Christ on His throne.

When Jesus Christ returns to set up His millennial kingdom, believers throughout all of history will rule with Him, seated with Him on His throne: "To him who overcomes I will grant to sit with Me on My throne, as I also overcame and sat down with My Father on His throne" (Revelation 3:21). Just as the church (you and I) has responsibility for the gospel of Jesus kingdom on earth now, you will have responsibility as a ruler in eternity with Christ. We have already seen that you will judge nations and the world itself. The Word also reveals a special authority given to the apostles. Jesus shared this concept with His disciples in Matthew and Luke, where He described their place on twelve thrones judging the twelve tribes of Israel.[8]

We know Scripture reveals that when you are in Christ, you are a new creation (see 2 Corinthians 5:17) and you are seated in glory with Him. Ephesians tells us that He "raised us up together, and made us sit together in the heavenly places in Christ Jesus" (2:6). You take your rightful place as an overcomer in Jesus Christ with Him in His rulership in the kingdom. As 2 Timothy says, "If we endure, we shall also reign with Him" (2:12). Friend, this is an amazing promise to you!

You will be heir of all things and God's child.

Inheriting all things means just that: everything in existence. This final and most extravagant promise is awarded to you by virtue of your relationship with Christ: "He who overcomes shall inherit all things, and I will be his God and he shall be My son" (Revelation 21:7).

This promise of being joint heirs of all that Christ possesses is echoed throughout the New Testament. For instance, John 1:12 explains that "as many as received Him, to them He gave the right to become children of God, to those who believe in His name." Jesus, as the natural heir of God's inheritance, possesses the universe and all that is in it (see Hebrews 1:2). By virtue of your born-again life in Christ, you become a son (or daughter) as well. You are part of the family inheritance. "If children, then heirs—heirs of God and joint heirs with Christ, if indeed we suffer with Him, that we may also be glorified together" (Romans 8:17). Throughout the New Testament we see this promise of inheritance.[9] Peter wrote about "an inheritance incorruptible and undefiled and that does not fade away, reserved in heaven for you" (1 Peter 1:4).

Because you are a son or daughter, then you also share the riches of Christ's personal inheritance—it is written in His will, the New Testament. We have seen through Scripture that

Jesus is going to reward us by sharing in the inheritance of His authority and delegation over all creation. These promises are magnificent and exciting! The brilliance of your forever life is vividly reinforced in both the New and Old Testaments:

> Those who are wise shall shine like the brightness of the firmament, and those who turn many to righteousness like the stars forever and ever. (Daniel 12:3)

> [You] have redeemed us to God by Your blood out of every tribe and tongue and people and nation, and have made us kings and priests to our God; and we shall reign on the earth. (Revelation 5:9–10)

All the promises we have examined in this chapter, from receiving a white stone with our name written on it to ruling in authority with Christ, have one common theme, one qualifier to receiving these rewards: "to him who overcomes."[10] There is a qualification to receive these rewards, but they are attainable. In the next chapter, we will look closer at what the Bible says about overcoming to find out how we can receive these blessings in heaven.

TIME	TO	GATE	REMARK
10:00	HEAVEN	A10	DELAYED
10:02	HEAVEN	A03	ON-TIME
10:08	HEAVEN	A06	CANCELED
10:09	HEAVEN	A12	ON-TIME
10:12	HEAVEN	B07	ON-TIME
10:14	HEAVEN	B02	DELAYED
10:21	HEAVEN	H07	ON-TIME

Boarding

Whether I've been waiting for a long time or just arrived, whether I've been put on standby or am rushing to make a connecting flight, I always feel a sense of relief when the flight attendants call the group number on my ticket. It's a reassurance that there is a place for me on that plane and that I am going to get to where I want to go. Maybe your journey of following Christ has been full of detours or delays. You might think that your life won't earn you heavenly rewards. But that isn't true! God has a place for you in His kingdom.

My friend Stan is a man of great faith. He often challenges me and models what it looks like to follow Jesus. He related how he was at a ball game one summer and felt the tug of the Holy Spirit. It was a beautiful day, and he could have ignored the prompting and instead enjoyed the game. But he decided to be faithful and struck up a conversation with a man sitting nearby. This man had a tear tattooed on his cheek, a street sign often indicative of the person having killed someone. The conversation turned to matters of faith, and Stan shared his own walk of faith and the good news of Christ. As Stan began witnessing to the man, the man expressed that there was no hope of forgiveness for him because he had killed someone.

Immediately, the biblical story of King David came to Stan's mind. He replied, "God can save a murderer—and still mightily use him." He shared about the life of David and his disobedience in killing Uriah after David had committed adultery with Uriah's wife.[11] Stan told of David's repentance and restoration. The man he was witnessing to was greatly encouraged that he, like David, could be forgiven. He eagerly repented and gave his life to Jesus Christ.

Whether you are hesitant to witness because you aren't sure if God can use you or you feel that you can't be forgiven, be assured that God has prepared a place in eternity for everyone who believes. Anyone can come to faith in Christ, and anyone can start on the path to receiving rewards in eternity. It isn't too late for you to start today!

What Will You Do to Have Your Best Life in Eternity?

1. The parable of the minas shows that you will receive tangible rewards in heaven directly

proportional to the increase you bring with your life on earth. In what ways are you investing in the kingdom of God in your daily life? How does that speak to the amount of reward you can expect?

2. How does this chapter's depiction of heaven match (or differ from) your concept of heaven? Have you ever thought about heaven being a city in which you will live? How does that make you feel?

3. We serve the Lord because we love Him for what He's done for us. How does the reality of receiving rewards for a life that brings kingdom increase change your way of living, if at all?

4. If bringing increase in your life means storing up treasures in heaven, what can you change now to increase the treasures you are laying up there?

5. God rewarded faithful, increasing lives with rulership over cities. Why do you think God rewarded His servants in this fashion? What reward from this chapter are you most looking forward to receiving?

Chapter 5
To the One Who Overcomes

What you can become depends on what you can overcome.
—Anthony Douglas Williams

When you think of someone who has overcome, who comes to mind? It might be a great leader or historical figure. Perhaps it is an apostle or spiritual leader who stood against injustice and served the oppressed. Or maybe it's someone more personal, such as a family member or friend who has endured hardship and pushed through to win. Whoever you think of, I imagine that you look up to, admire, and would like to imitate their life. We look with admiration at those who endure war, famine, or other tribulations and not only survive but extend mercy and use the experience to seek justice for future generations. After reading the preceding chapter, it may not surprise you to learn that the Bible has something important to say about those who overcome. In fact, God has given many promises to overcomers. But how do you know for sure whether you fall into that category? To find out, let's turn to His Word.

Scripture tells us, "It is written: 'Eye has seen not seen, nor ear heard, nor have entered into the heart of man the things which God has prepared for those who love Him'" (1 Corinthians 2:9). In other words, you can't even *imagine* the things that God has for you in heaven. God is prepared to bless you beyond measure. He is waiting to show you the riches of His kindness—for eternity! In chapter 4 we talked about some of these rewards. They are indeed magnificent! You will:

- Live in a holy city and be in paradise eating from the tree of life
- Not be hurt by the second death
- Have spiritual food, a white stone, and a new name known by you and God
- Be given authority, even power over the nations
- Be clothed in white garments and have your name written in the Book of Life
- Get a personal introduction to God
- Have a permanent place in God's kingdom
- Be seated with Christ on His throne
- Be heir of all things and God's child

Preceding every one of these promises given in the book of Revelation is this phrase: "To him who *overcomes* I will give . . ." That's what this chapter is about: finding out exactly what it means to overcome, so we can reap the inconceivable rewards of heaven.

> **God is waiting to show you the riches of His kindness—for eternity!**

These rewards are incomprehensibly good. Just being saved and getting into heaven is awesome, but to know that you potentially also have these rewards waiting for you is beyond blessing and reflects God's kindness. Scripture even tells us this is God's intention—He is waiting to show you abundant goodness beyond your wildest dreams, "that in the ages to come He might show the exceeding riches of His grace in His kindness toward us in Christ Jesus" (Ephesians 2:7).

So how do you know whether these "exceeding riches" are for you? These magnificent rewards of heaven are conditional, but the good news is that we're told the requirements we need to meet. These rewards are promised to you for eternity if you do. They're fully dependent—every single one of them—on one thing: overcoming.

Still, at the risk of being redundant, let's be clear: you don't get into heaven by overcoming. Jesus already gained entrance for you into His kingdom when He overcame sin and death on the cross of Calvary. He gave you that by faith, which means that *He* earned your salvation—not you. In John 16:33 Jesus told us, "I have overcome the world." He is the ultimate overcomer! When you place your faith in Him, you are already assured a place in eternity with Him. Jesus overcame for your salvation because of His great love for you. This is good news for those of us who truly desire to overcome. Yet the rewards you receive in heaven are predicated on your works—not Jesus' works. So it's important to see exactly what Scripture says about overcoming so that you can follow this command, as it will impact your heavenly life for billions of years in eternity.

Overcoming implies effort on behalf of the overcomer. *You* have a part to play in overcoming. You are the one who has to do it—it depends on you and your intentionality. The experience you will have in your forever life in heaven depends entirely on how you live your life here on earth

> **The quality of your forever life in heaven depends on how you live your life here on earth.**

and whether your works are founded in Jesus. This is the essence of what it means to overcome—to live a life that is worthy to earn rewards for Jesus name. This is the great promise of those who have done well: eternal life! Romans 2:7 promises "eternal life to those who by patient continuance in doing good seek for glory, honor, and immortality."

Now that we've established the importance of overcoming to produce good works and earn heavenly blessings, you may be wondering exactly *how* you can overcome. What is God's definition of *overcoming*? What is the key to living in a way that honors our Lord Jesus Christ? To find the answer, let's dig into Scripture. God has laid out clear instructions in His Word that are intended to guide us and give tangible action steps. The process of overcoming isn't meant to be a mystery. As we look at overcoming in the Bible, we will see God's plan for how we should live on earth.

Before we dive in, it's helpful to recall that the New Testament was originally written in Koine Greek. The Greek word that translates as *overcome* is used twenty-eight times in the New Testament. The flavor of the meaning is the same throughout: "to overcome, conquer, prevail, get the victory."[1] Specifically, it implies a battle. There is a sense of attaining mastery over the world, the flesh, and the devil. This theme of both earthly and spiritual warfare carries throughout the following passages and is an important component to understanding the biblical definition—and informs us on how to overcome.

Tucked away in Revelation 12 we find the secret to overcoming revealed in one powerful verse, which specifically tells how to bring increase. God is so kind as to give us these instructions in the last book of the Bible: "And they overcame him by the *blood of the Lamb* and by the *word of their testimony*, and they *did not love their lives to the death*" (v. 11, emphasis mine). Here we find three elements of overcoming:

1. You overcome by the blood of the Lamb. This means that you have fully accepted the atoning sacrifice of your Lord Jesus Christ. Overcoming rests on the sovereign finished work of Christ on the cross. He earned salvation for you, and you receive it by faith alone and enter into heaven. This sets you up and makes you eligible to be blessed and hear "well done."

2. You overcome by the word of your testimony. Your witness for Jesus is tantamount to living a life that will earn eternal rewards. Your words and actions come into play here. Jesus blood provides you and me with right standing—it sets us up and gives us a platform to live an overcoming life. However, the verse goes on to show that overcoming also requires a sacrificial life of biblical action in both word (your testimony) and deed.

3. You overcome by loving not your life to the death. This selflessness is the natural result of personally assimilating what Jesus has done for you and simply refers to responding by living a holy life that is faithful to the end in your earthly journey. When you do, you receive "the crown of righteousness" (Revelation 2:10; see also 2 Timothy 4:6–8).

The first and third requirements to overcoming are related to spiritual and sacrificial actions. The middle one relates directly to our testimony. We will look at that closer in the next chapter. Regarding the spiritual and sacrificial aspects of what it means to overcome, here are a few biblical keys to overcoming.

Overcoming is being "born of God."

According to Scripture, the first step to overcoming is being born again. As a Christian, you may describe yourself or others as "born-again" without thinking through what you are referring to.

Biblically, what does it mean to be "born of God," and what does this concept have to do with overcoming? The apostle John was the one who used this language. He documented Jesus' conversation with Nicodemus, which began with a question. Nicodemus approached Jesus and asked, "How can a man be born when he is old? Can he enter a second time into his mother's womb and be born?" Jesus replied, "Unless one is born again, he cannot see the kingdom of God" (John 3:3). We know from context and their further conversation that Jesus was talking about spiritual rebirth as a requirement for entering heaven. While this initially appears to be a conversation about salvation rather than earning eternal rewards through overcoming, 1 John 5:4 gives insight into the relationship between the two: "For whatever is born of God overcomes the world. And this is the victory that has overcome the world—our faith." We will look at the faith aspect in the last half of this verse shortly. But let's look at this born-again aspect of overcoming. As a born-again believer, not only will you enter into the kingdom, but you also can overcome the temptations and troubles of this world, all because you are "born of God." Friends, this is good news for all believers! We see this in 1 John 5:1, which tells us that "whoever believes that Jesus is the Christ is born of God." That means you and me!

There is a reason that Jesus chose this particular metaphor. Rather than giving an overly spiritual answer to Nicodemus,

He chose to compare salvation to a physical process (birth), reminding us that the physical work of the cross redeems our bodies as well as our souls. Our whole being matters to God. Jesus showed this when He distinguished further in verse 5 that we must be born both of "water and the Spirit." The water refers to the natural birthing process. Being born of the Spirit is being born by faith—becoming one spirit with God. "But he who is joined to the Lord is one spirit with Him" (1 Corinthians 6:17). Being born again means that we die to our fleshly desires and are made new—heart, body, mind, and soul. Ultimately, it is evident that we have to *experience* this new birth to overcome—not in the literal physical sense, but in terms of committing all of who we are to Christ. Is that our testimony? Beyond an intellectual understanding of who Jesus is, can we say we are truly born again?

John then went on to say that "whoever has been born of God does not sin . . . because he has been born of God" (1 John 3:9). In this passage there's an element of mastering sin in your life because of your born-again relationship with God. While this doesn't mean that you will never sin again, it does mean that you are seen as holy before God because of your faith placed in Jesus finished work on the cross. Because you have been redeemed, you should *want* to personally strive to overcome the sin in the world like Jesus did. He already provided the perfect example of a sinless life: "[Jesus] was in all points tempted as we are, yet without sin" (Hebrews 4:15). John specifically defined what it means to overcome "the world" in 1 John 2:16–17, when he said, "For all that is in the world—the lust of the flesh, the lust of the eyes, and the pride of life—is not of the Father but is of the world. And the world is passing away, and the lust of it; but he who does the will of God abides forever." Your denying worldly lusts and pride is an important component of overcoming, that you may reap rewards in your forever life. If you truly love Jesus and are striving to deny sin, following His example, you will live in His kingdom for eternity!

On the other hand, God's Word details that if we are overcome by sin, we are a slave to that sin. We learn this in 2 Peter 2:19: "For by whom a person is overcome, by him also he is brought into bondage" (emphasis mine). So, the ever-present battle lines are either: sin will overcome us or we will overcome it. There is no middle ground when it comes to the issue of overcoming, which is why having a biblical understanding of this concept is so important to the way we live on earth.

> **Faith is key to the overcoming life.**

"For whatever is born of God overcomes the world. And this is the victory that has overcome the world—our faith" (1 John 5:4). John summed up the victory of overcoming by joining our born-again experience to exercising our faith. Paul wrote that without faith we cannot even please God and continued to chronicle the heroes of the faith who moved mountains, conquered armies, and had various other victories by faith (see Hebrews 11). All of these that were described in this chapter were pre-resurrection believers—they were not born again. This is where you and I have such a great advantage as born-again Christians! Not only are we born again into being new creatures in Christ (see 2 Corinthians 5:17), but we also are able to exercise the same faith in God that strengthened the champions described in the Old Testament. I would say so boldly and in agreement with Jesus Himself that the least in the born-again kingdom of Jesus Christ is greater than all of the Old Testament saints. Jesus made the comparison with John the Baptist, whom He said was carrying the spirit of Elijah (see Matthew 11:14; Luke 1:17). But then He said that the least in the kingdom of God is greater than John, and John was more than a prophet (see Matthew 11:9, 11). So that means that the believer—you and I—are more than the prophets and John the Baptist! How can this be? It's because before the resurrection they overcame by faith alone. For you and me, we add to our faith the addition of being filled with the Holy Spirit, having the Word of God in writing, and having and becoming new creatures in Jesus Christ—being born again through faith.

This is really good news! Each one of us, at best, is flawed and sinful. Yet we know "if we confess our sins, He is faithful and just to forgive us our sins and to cleanse us from all unrighteousness" (1 John 1:9). This is because of the finished work of Jesus on Calvary, which the Old Testament saints neither understood nor could access. But we have the ability to instantly overcome all of Satan's attacks and our failures by placing our faith in the finished work of Jesus Christ, whom Scripture says will one day present us blameless before God's presence. Regardless of the sin you may have done, God honors a repentant heart, and you can know fully that you are forgiven and set free. This is why He describes faith as a breastplate protecting our heart (see 1 Thessalonians 5:8). By faith we master sin in our lives.

Second Peter 2:20 says, "For if, after they have escaped the pollutions of the world through the knowledge of the Lord and Savior Jesus Christ, they are again entangled in them and *overcome*, the latter end is worse for them than the beginning" (emphasis mine). Scripture uses a different word for *overcoming* in this verse—that is, for sin overcoming us.[2] Here *overcome* carries a sense of inferiority. In this context, rather than actively working to overcome, we are passive recipients of the natural consequences of our sin nature—we are controlled by our own desires. It is the opposite of the term for *overcoming* that we find tied to our rewards in Revelation—one that means "mastery." It all comes down to this question: Who is the master of your life? Your born-again nature or your sin nature?

An example of the conflict can be portrayed as two dogs, one representing your sin nature and the other your born-again nature. The black dog is your sin nature. The white dog is your born-again nature. They are in conflict. The question of which one wins is simple. It's the one that is given the most food. "Starve" the black dog in your life, your sin nature; deny it continually. Feed continually your born-again nature.

We see this tension described in Romans as well, from the apostle Paul himself. Paul was a champion of the Bible, and his conversion story is truly remarkable.[3] He was the man who wrote most of the New Testament, yet he still struggled with his sin nature. Listen to how he described it: "For I delight in the law of God according to the inward man. But I see another law in my members, warring against the law of my mind, and bringing me into captivity to the law of sin which is in my members. O wretched man that I am!" (Romans 7:22–24). We never outgrow warfare; we simply must learn to fight.

Even Paul, who was shipwrecked, stoned, and imprisoned for his faith, faced this spiritual battle between the "law of God" and "law of sin," which we as believers are still waging today. To overcome is not to be free from this struggle, but instead to place your trust in God and remind yourself that He has already won. When He is first in your life, you can overcome despite your sin nature since you have been redeemed. You belong to Him. Because Jesus took the penalty for your sin and set you free from the curse of Adam, Scripture exhorts you to strive to live an overcoming life worthy of the Lord, which pleases Him. In particular, we see this in Colossians 1:10, which calls us to "walk worthy of the Lord, fully pleasing Him, being fruitful in every good work and increasing in the knowledge of God." You have been liberated to overcome. There is evidence all through Scripture that faith is a vital quality to living a life characterized by victory.

Scripture is packed with stories that show this principle—that your strongest weapon in overcoming is faith-filled obedience to God's Word. For example, Joshua was told to conquer the first heavily guarded city, Jericho, not by reasoned military strategy but by simply obeying God's commands.[4] We know that faith comes by hearing and obeying the Word of God. Your willingness to step out and act on God's promises in faith, like Joshua, gives you the ability not just to overcome yourself, but to conquer kingdoms—and even overcome the world![5]

> **Your strongest weapon in overcoming is simple obedience to God's Word.**

Like the instructions given to Joshua, God's directions to you may not necessarily make sense. Sometimes obedience is like that—it requires a step of faith. You don't have to understand the purposes behind God's plan to do His will—it just requires your humility to listen, follow, and let Him do the work. You can trust that He knows what He is doing and has good plans for you.

God did the work for Joshua to show His glory; He collapsed the walls of Jericho. In 1997 two Italian archaeologists were hired by the Palestinian department of archaeology and excavated for one month at ancient Jericho. Their conclusion was not surprising to those of us who believe Scripture. Surrounding the entire city, the archaeologists found an enormous earthen embankment with huge stone retaining walls at its base. At the top of the embankment also stood a forty-six-foot wall, and houses were actually built on this massive wall. The Bible says that the wall "fell down flat" (Joshua 6:20). The archaeologists found piles of mud and bricks from the collapsed wall, confirming the wall was not destroyed or knocked down by a battering ram but had collapsed. One portion of the wall, though, was still standing. This may have been the location of Rahab's house.[6]

The same miraculous power that collapsed the wall of Jericho is available to you today. By faith you can get blessings you don't deserve, favor you haven't earned, solutions you can't figure out, and deliverance from circumstances beyond your control. God specializes and is glorified in resolving your hopeless situations! Friend, when you overcome, your faith grows and you earn heavenly rewards. God wants you to exercise your faith in His Word. He cares about your personal circumstances and wants you to overcome in the pressing issues of life—not to be overcome by them. Let's explore two very similar examples from Scripture.

> God is glorified in resolving your hopeless situations!

In 2 Kings 4 we find another story where faith in the face of dire circumstances leads to overcoming. A woman was married to one of Elisha's fellow prophets (servants). But her husband died, and she was left a widow with two sons. She was also left with a pile of debt that she could not pay. There seemed to be no way out of her situation. The creditors were coming to sell her sons into slavery to pay the debt. She was desperate and likely feeling overcome by her circumstances. But her faith had the final word!

The prophet Elisha heard about her dilemma and how she was going to lose her sons to her debtors. So he gave her a word from God: "Go, borrow vessels from everywhere, from all your neighbors—empty vessels; do not gather just a few" (v. 3). God was about to work a miracle. She had just one small vessel of oil in her house, constituting her entire earthly possessions. But a little with God is an abundance if it's met with faith in His Word. So she followed Elisha's command and gathered empty vessels. As she poured her little bit of oil into each vessel, they completely filled up, and she had enough to pay off her creditors. She definitely had the oil of gladness!

This is an example of what God wants to accomplish in your life. He wants you to overcome your circumstances and be free through faith in His Word. Rather than barely scraping by, God wants to fill your life with blessings. It is His desire to reward your faith by not only helping you overcome your circumstances, but by giving you the opportunity to flourish with great joy. It is interesting that the widow's story is very similar to another difficult circumstance found in the New Testament—and the setup of Jesus first miracle.

Like the widow's story found in 2 Kings, Jesus first miracle (proving that He was as mighty as the prophet Elisha) also involved filling empty vessels. This miracle was performed to meet a difficult personal need at a wedding in Cana. The hosts of the event (friends of Jesus mother, Mary) had run out of wine. What may seem minor to you was an issue of hospitality and meant a great deal in Jesus cultural context. The situation was a significant embarrassment to His mother and her friends.

Although they had run out of wine, they did have empty vessels—large ones. What seems large, empty, and hopeless to us is full of potential and blessing with God! Jesus ordered that the empty vessels be filled with water. This may not have seemed particularly reasonable, as they needed wine not water. Yet in obedience, the servants filled the jars to the brim. Then Jesus commanded them to take the water from the vessels and present it to the master of the feast. This was even more unreasonable! The master of the feast was expecting wine, so to bring him water instead was adding insult to injury. Yet amid that stress, they obeyed, and their faith was rewarded with a miracle—the water was turned into the best of wine. Their faith-filled obedience overcame their circumstances through the power of God to bring blessing.

Again, here we see the extravagant goodness of God. He turned the widow's and the couple's desperate situations into experiences of breakout *abundance*. Overcoming is not just prevailing in a hard-won fight, friend; rather, in your life it leads to a place of victory and abundant blessing beyond just your need. God intends to show this extravagant favor to those who dare to move forth in faith on His revealed Word.

The marriage, or wine, miracle was not a life-and-death matter, but it's interesting that Jesus chose to simply deal with a difficult personal circumstance for His first miracle. This is encouraging because it shows that He cares about your individual struggles, and it gives you hope to overcome them. God delights in making hopeless circumstances the means by which He can display His glory for your benefit if you exercise faith and obedience in His Word. The point is simple and very encouraging: if you obey God's Word in your circumstances (no matter how hopeless), you can have victory and overcome by faith. You will be greatly rewarded for your obedience.

Overcoming is conquering evil.

We've seen that overcoming is only possible through faith. This is because faith is the antithesis of the devil's plan for your life. The Enemy's desire is the opposite of faith; it is fear, which can be described by this acronym:

False
Evidence
Appearing
Real

Faith is fearless because faith comes by hearing the Word of God, and God's Word is greater than any fear or device of Satan. We are called to expose the deeds of darkness: "Have no fellowship with the unfruitful works of darkness, but rather expose them" (Ephesians 5:11). The overcoming life is at war with evil and the satanic world's system. When you act in faith, you not only are able to overcome your circumstances but are also able to overcome evil. There is great power in a life characterized by overcoming. Romans 12:21 tells us, "Do not be overcome by evil, but overcome evil with good." God has given you a way to overcome!

God has destined you to overcome Satan's trespassing in your life. There's a theme here in overcoming, which puts you in opposition with the world. We know that Satan is "the prince of the power of the air, the spirit who now works in the sons of disobedience" (Ephesians 2:2). You must keep your life (your palace, in the following analogy) from his power: "When a strong man, fully armed, guards his own palace, his goods are in peace. But when a stronger than he comes upon him and overcomes him, he takes from him all his armor in which he trusted, and divides his spoils" (Luke 11:21–22). This verse is the fulfillment of Jesus description of Satan's motives, which are "to steal, and to kill, and to destroy" (John 10:10). You must remain steadfastly vigilant to oppose him in this. We know that the Enemy is seeking to conquer us. First Peter 5:8–9 describes this with the analogy of a lion: "Your adversary the devil walks about like a roaring lion, seeking whom he may devour. Resist him, steadfast in the faith." While this image may be alarming at first, remember that you truly have nothing to fear when you are in Christ. You are destined to overcome. John told us specifically that part of overcoming is having victory over the wicked one, Satan, in our lives: "I write to you, fathers, because you have known Him who is from the beginning. I write to you, young men, because you have overcome the wicked one. I write to you, little children, because you have known the Father" (1 John 2:13).

When you choose to deny your worldly desires, you are, overcoming! Yet, in doing that, your decision puts you in contest with Satan. But 1 John goes on to show that we have great assurance. The indwelling presence of the Holy Spirit in your life is greater than the arrows of the Enemy and enables you to defeat Satan. We see this in 1 John 4:4, which says, "You are of God, little children, and have overcome them, because He who is in you is greater than he who is in the world." The presence of Jesus in your life and the Holy Spirit *in you* gives you authority over sin and the devil. You are called to destroy Satan's strongholds in your life once and for all. We see this in the Scripture that says, "For this purpose the Son of God was manifested, that He might destroy the works of the devil" (1 John 3:8). Jesus said, "As the Father has sent Me, I also send you" (John 20:21). The good news is that you are able to have victory over Satan's work in your life! He has no power over you.

> To overcome requires self-denial.

I encourage you to exercise this authority, which God has given you, over Satan in your life today. Declare it: "Today I take authority over you, Satan, in Jesus Christ, and evict you and your stronghold over my life because greater is Jesus than I—and greater than you and your attacks."

Overcoming happens because you are called, chosen, and faithful.

Not only do you overcome evil through faith in Jesus, but you do so because of your identity as a child of God who is called to a specific purpose. We see this in Revelation 17:14, which states,

"These will make war with the Lamb, and the Lamb will overcome them, for He is Lord of lords and King of kings; and *those who are with Him are called, chosen, and faithful*" (emphasis mine). This verse speaks of Christ's (the Lamb's) final return and His ultimate victory over Satan and all his followers. What's really amazing is that you're included in the battle! It says, "Those who are with Him are called, chosen, and faithful"—that, my friend, is the body of Christ: you and me. In your calling and faithfulness in Jesus, you contribute to and share in that victory. This reflects the ultimate overcoming privilege of those who are in Christ. You don't need to worry about the outcome—you have already overcome! God's Word tells us that "if anyone is in Christ, he is a new creation; old things have passed away; behold, all things have become new" (2 Corinthians 5:17). We know that God chose believers "before the foundation of the world" (Ephesians 1:4). We also know that "these He also called; whom He called, these He also justified; and whom He justified, these He also glorified" (Romans 8:30). You are a new creation, chosen by God to reveal His glory. God is on His throne, and you are invited into His everlasting kingdom. These verses are talking about Christians—you and me!

Paul prayed that we would "walk worthy of the Lord, fully pleasing Him" (Colossians 1:10). Here we see the sovereignty of God—calling you and choosing you—as well as your part in being faithful. In the words of the Paul, "I have fought the good fight, I have finished the race, I have kept the faith. Finally, there is laid up for me the crown of righteousness, which the Lord, the righteous Judge, will give to me on that Day, and not to me only but also to all who have loved His appearing" (2 Timothy 4:7–8). Again, the reward of a

> **To overcome is lifelong faithfulness to your call.**

crown is given to you when you are faithful throughout your life. Heavenly blessings await.

Overcoming is the sovereignty of God working with the will of man.

Overcoming is based first on faith that God is at work in and through you and that His sovereign will is accomplished. You are able to overcome because He already has! We see this throughout Scripture: "These things I have spoken to you, that in Me you may have peace. In the world you will have tribulation; but be of good cheer, I have overcome the world" (John 16:33). The word *world* is the Greek word *kosmos*, which includes all of creation—universe, world systems, people, affairs of life.[7] Jesus has conquered the world—all of it! And we share in that victory, overcoming by faith in His sovereign finished work. You do not need to fear death because you have been given the assurance of abundant heavenly rewards and a place in God's kingdom, where you will be eternally blessed!

> **Your testimony of Jesus is the evidence and essence of overcoming.**

While you can never repay the gift that Jesus has freely given, you reciprocate His finished work by willingly dedicating your life to His testimony and holiness. Your testimony of Jesus is the evidence and essence of overcoming. Jesus Himself, in the Sermon on the Mount, affirmed that holy living requires good works: "Let your light so shine before men, that they may see your good works and glorify your Father in heaven" (Matthew 5:16). Note that your good works are not intended for your own benefit but to lead others to the Lord. This is an act of worship. Jesus again spoke this important truth in Matthew 7:21, saying, "Not everyone who says to Me, 'Lord, Lord,' shall enter the kingdom of heaven, but he *who does the will of My Father* in heaven" (emphasis mine). Jesus has instructed you to walk out your faith in daily, practical conformity to His Word. He identified His true disciples by this principle: "If you abide in My word, you are My disciples indeed. And you shall know the truth, and the truth shall make you free" (John 8:31–32).

As we will see, your good works, loving not your life until the day you die, and your testimony of Jesus are the evidence and essence of overcoming faith.

> **A faith-filled, self-denying life that testifies of Jesus Christ gains victory!**

It is the overcoming life as a result of lived-out faith that receives the richest rewards of heaven and the praise "well done." We have seen in this chapter that the rich rewards awaiting us in heaven are tied to and dependent—every one of them—on our ability to overcome. We examined the many facets of overcoming: that it requires effort, that we must be born again, and that we overcome sin and evil through faith-filled obedience to our calling. We simply must learn to fight against the world, our flesh, and the devil. Applying these principles is the key that opens the door to heaven's richest blessings.

Hidden in Revelation 12, God has revealed the clearest secret to living the type of life that will unlock eternal rewards, which we will see in the following chapter. We will examine some simple ways to live this out in the world around us and explore this secret fully. To the degree that you can apply these biblical instructions, your rewards in heaven will be truly great!

TIME	TO	GATE	REMARK
10:00	HEAVEN	A10	DELAYED
10:02	HEAVEN	A03	ON-TIME
10:08	HEAVEN	A06	CANCELED
10:09	HEAVEN	A12	ON-TIME
10:12	HEAVEN	B07	ON-TIME
10:14	HEAVEN	B02	DELAYED
10:21	HEAVEN	H07	ON-TIME

Takeoff

There are certain requirements for a flight to leave the ground. The engine needs fuel, the pilot needs correct coordinates, and the crew needs to perform specific tasks in preparation. As passengers, it is our job to listen to the flight attendants, stow our bags, and fasten our seat belts. In the same way, you need spiritual fuel (biblical teaching), direction (from the Holy Spirit), and community with other believers to ensure that you follow your pilot's (God's) commands. It is your job to put aside any obstacles that would hinder you, and fasten your heart and mind on Jesus. Sadly, many people live their entire lives without achieving spiritual takeoff.

One man in particular comes to mind. I had boarded my flight, and shortly after I was seated, a polished businessman in his forties took the seat to my left. As the flight ensued, we engaged in a conversation regarding his career. It turns out that he was a national marketing director for a large food chain. In worldly terms, he appeared successful, but during our conversation, I could tell that he knew something was missing in his life. As the conversation continued and I built rapport with him, I shot a thought prayer to the Lord: "Heavenly Father, is there anything You would have me say to this man?" This verse came to my mind: "What will it profit a man if he gains the whole world, and loses his own soul?" (Mark 8:36).

So I told the guy sitting next to me, "You know, one thing that really baffles me is that we go to college, plan our career, plan our family, plan our retirement, and then comes that fateful day—which all of us shall surely face—where we step over that line, the line into eternity, and we've made no plans for this inescapable eventuality. It doesn't make sense! What does it profit a man if he gains the whole world and loses his soul?"

To my surprise, he said, "You know, I've thought about that recently—it's funny that you say that."

I said, "Well, I believe it was from the Lord. Do you have any spiritual beliefs?"

He told me that he prays every now and then when he's in trouble. I said, "We all do that, but that's different from having an ongoing relationship where Jesus Christ, the King of kings, holds control over our decisions and life goals—that He's our Lord."

This opened the opportunity for me to share the gospel with him. Your testimony is powerful too, and sharing it is the only way that you are able to live an overcoming life that will bring eternal rewards.

What Will You Do to Have Your Best Life in Eternity?

1. How did Jesus explain the concept of being born again to Nicodemus? What does it mean to be reborn spiritually? Can you honestly say you have experienced being born again?

2. Consider the stories of the widow and Jesus first miracle. In what ways has God blessed you with abundance? In what areas of need can you increase your faith so that you can experience His overflowing blessings in your own life?

3. Revelation 17:14 tells us that we are "called, chosen, and faithful." Which of these is the most meaningful to you? Is there one that you have yet to embrace?

4. Consider those in your life (family, work, etc.) who may not have repented and received Jesus. How can you share your testimony with them?

5. In what ways are you living out your faith? Are there areas in your life needing victory where you can ask God to help you overcome?

Chapter 6
Revelation's Secret to Hearing "Well Done"

What we do now echoes in eternity.
—Marcus Aurelius

Father God deeply desires to tell you, "Well done," and to richly reward you for living an overcoming, faithful life on earth. As we saw in chapter 4, His blessings, which await your heavenly reality, truly will be better than your wildest imagination. We also saw in the previous chapters that God has structured all of creation with this purpose in mind: that you might overcome in this life, arrive in heaven, meet His approval as your works are tested by fire and found to be fine gold, and reap incredible rewards for eternity. God has done His part . . . He has set you up to overcome through sending Jesus to Calvary. Now you must do your part.

In arriving at this point in our journey together, we have seen that the biblical assurance of hearing "well done," having your life's work tested, and receiving wonderful heavenly rewards all depend on two things:

1. Your life bringing increase through stewardship of the Lord's entrustment, discussed in chapter 2.

2. Overcoming through faith-filled obedience to God's Word as discussed in chapter 5.

God desires to bless you and wants to be sure you will meet these requirements, so He gave you an easily understandable verse. We looked at part of this important verse in the previous chapter. Now let's look at the final requirement to overcome:

They overcame by . . . the word of their testimony. (Revelation 12:11)

It is significant that this verse tells us that the "word of [our] testimony" is an essential aspect of overcoming. We are directly involved in the process! This is a challenge to us as believers. We must overcome our worldly loves and fears, instead increasing God's kingdom by testifying about Jesus redemptive work in our life. Romans 10:9 says, "If you confess with your mouth the Lord Jesus and believe in your heart that God has raised Him from the dead, you will be saved." We know that "out of the . . . heart his mouth speaks" (Luke 6:45). That is why we must never be ashamed of the testimony of our faith in and love for Jesus Christ. This is consistent with the Great Commission in Matthew 28 and the activity of the disciples after Jesus left earth. It is God's plan for how He will build His church—through you and me. Your testimony is the secret to a kingdom-relevant life that God will commend and abundantly reward.

> **Jesus' blood allows you to live an overcoming life.**

Friend, how you live here cannot be erased. You will live with it throughout eternity! Living by faith alone is not the complete will of God. It's clear throughout Scripture that God expects you to live a holy life *after* you're saved. To overcome is to have victory over your sin nature, not just for personal comfort but also for God's purpose. This is what "loved not their lives unto the death" refers to (Revelation 12:11 KJV). Kingdom fruitfulness is God's will for you and is pleasing to Him: "That you may walk worthy of the Lord, fully pleasing Him, being fruitful in every good work and increasing in the knowledge of God" (Colossians 1:10).

Bearing good fruit throughout life is God's plan for you. The verse in Colossians says that you should be filled with the "knowledge of God" so that you can bear good fruit. How can you know God's will? One way is by studying His Word and applying it to your life. You can also pray earnestly and listen for His still small voice to convict your conscience or motivate you toward action. What it all comes down to is truly loving Him. To be filled, your heart must be all in. Only then can you fulfill the eternal plans God has for you.

We know that God is concerned with matters of the heart, not outward appearances. Jesus consistently praised those who gave out of love or honestly confessed their sins rather than those like the Pharisees who desired to *appear* holy. We also see this in God's selection of David amid his bigger brothers. God isn't concerned with who seems the most successful. Rather, He is looking to see if your heart is wholly committed to Him. Second Chronicles 16:9 explains, "For the eyes of the LORD run to and fro throughout the whole earth, to show Himself strong on behalf of those whose heart is loyal to Him." God is actively seeking out those who belong to Him—people like you and me! He wants to greatly bless our acts of faithfulness.

But there is a problem with our heart being completely His. We find in Jeremiah 17:9–10: "The heart is deceitful above all things, and desperately wicked; who can know it? I, the

LORD, search the heart, I test the mind, even to give every man according to his ways, according to the fruit of his doings." While God knows your inner workings and is able to search you, you may be blind to your own faults and shortcomings. Your intentions, presuppositions, misguided teachings, and perceptions may obscure whether your heart is all in for Jesus. So how can you know if your heart is all in? What are the markers of someone who is truly committed to Christ?

> How can you know if your heart is all in?

A heart that is fully committed is one filled with love for God. Such a person can't help but share that love with others. We have an example from one of Jesus disciples in the first days of the early church that is particularly poignant. Listen to Peter's defense when commanded by the Pharisees not to testify about Jesus: "For we cannot but speak the things which we have seen and heard" (Acts 4:20). Peter's and John's hearts were so overflowing with love for Jesus and excitement over the gift of eternal life, they couldn't help but talk about it!

In Luke 6:45 Jesus Himself said, "Out of the abundance of the heart his mouth speaks." Scripture makes clear that your day-to-day conversations reveal what fills your heart. Is it your delight to speak of the things of this world or the things of Jesus kingdom? An eagerness to tell others of your love for Jesus is an accurate measurement of what fills your heart and the level of your commitment to kingdom purposes. Ultimately, your speech reveals the treasures of your heart.

With that in mind, I have a legitimate question for you: Are you in love—like really in love today—with the One who runs heaven, the place where you hope to spend your eternity? He is, after all, the One on the throne. He made heaven for you, and He gave His all so that you might enjoy it. He is the One you must please if you hope to receive rewards and hear, "Well done, good and faithful servant." Take a moment to consider, what do your daily actions reveal about the state of your heart?

The most intimate, fulfilling aspect of your life can be—and should be—your relationship with a faithful God, your true Father. His love makes your life complete with assurance and purpose. Your destiny is to be with Him forever. This heart-full relationship should compel you, with eager desire, to share this treasure with others. What is the most important thing to Jesus Christ? The greatest desire of His heart is for you to tell others about His love for them. We know this to be true by His own words.

> **Your speech reveals the treasure of your heart.**

There are rare defining moments in life when words are extremely important. For example, I think of the game show *Who Wants to Be a Millionaire?* The contestants are asked the question upon which thousands, perhaps tens of thousands, of dollars are contingent: "Is that your final answer?" The outcome of the contestants' words determines whether they win or lose. Even more life-changing are the covenantal words found in marriage vows. The words "I do" spoken to your bride or groom ushers in the unfolding, the beginning of a couple, a home, a new life—perhaps a new family and an existence together for decades to come. All of this is confirmed by two simple words. Words are valuable indeed.

One of the most definitive times when words are important is the moment when a person speaks the final words of their life—their "last words," if you will. Often, they are spoken in the waning hours of a person's sickness, whispered into the longing, anxious ears of a beloved spouse, son, or daughter. Most would agree that, if physically or mentally able, their last words will be carefully chosen. They are meant to leave instructions and a last expression of the deepest emotions of one's heart.

I think Jesus last words were no different. The message that Jesus left with His disciples before He departed into heaven was *deliberately* chosen. He knew these would be His final recorded words, and I believe that these words were the deepest and most profound expression of the heart of our Lord. They also hold the most certain secret to our blessing and hearing "well done."

On what would be His last day on earth before His ascension (found in Acts 1), Jesus spoke to His disciples from the Mount of Olives. Right before He ascended into heaven, He told them, "*You shall be witnesses to Me* in Jerusalem, and in all Judea and Samaria, and to the end of the earth" (Acts 1:8, emphasis mine). With these parting words, Jesus left the earth, not to return again until He comes back on that glorious day at the consummation of all creation and human history.

Should you take these final words as just another expression by Jesus? I would strongly contend that this is Jesus most important command to His disciples, and by extension to you and me. Wouldn't His last words, spoken at the conclusion of His earthly ministry and the threshold of the church age, express the summation and priority of all that His ministry was meant to be? Wouldn't this be the capstone, the last "marching order" to you, His follower, from the captain of your faith?

> **Jesus' last words on earth give you the secret to overcoming.**

Jesus final instruction is the surest secret to hearing the words "well done, good and faithful servant." It is the key to bringing kingdom-relevant *increase* in your life. As I mentioned earlier, these words are the indicator as to whether the good works of your earthly life will be evaluated in heaven as gold, silver, and precious stones. Jesus last words on earth give you the secret to overcoming. He was so gracious to give you the secret so simply and pointedly. He did this as the last clear expression of His ministry, because His greatest desire is to give you the ability to overcome, hear "well done," and enjoy the rewards of heaven with Him. That is why Jesus chose those specific words. Friend, He wants to bless you and see you succeed!

It is no coincidence that following the recording of Jesus life on earth through the Gospels (Matthew, Mark, Luke, and John), the next book of the Bible is the *Acts* of the apostles, testifying about Him! Through obedience to His final command, the apostles were able to live fearlessly, overcoming circumstances of all kinds because they "did not love their lives to the death" (Revelation 12:11). Their lives are an inspiration and witness to us today. They were simple fishermen and workers, but through obeying Jesus command to testify of what they'd seen and how He had changed their lives, they ignited the early church and sparked a movement that continues to spread across the globe today. God planted them in a specific time and place to exponentially grow His followers and bring kingdom increase. Little children, it is the Father's delight to give you the keys to the kingdom. The key is our testimony of Jesus!

> **Little children, it is the Father's delight to give you the keys to the kingdom.**

Ultimately, we have seen that Jesus greatest desire is for you to be His witness. The greatest obstacle you must overcome in your Christian experience is to move beyond words to *act* on your deeply held values, putting works to your faith. While this may be difficult at first and does not always come easily, it is imperative that you as a believer testify about Jesus finished work on the cross and the message of salvation. This should be done as an expression of your love to and for Him. In other words, your love for Jesus should compel you to share that love with others!

With His last words in Acts 1:8, Jesus got very personal. He said, "*You* shall be witnesses to *Me*" (emphasis mine). He didn't say the church. He didn't say the pastor. He didn't say some missionary or itinerant evangelist—He said that *you and I* will be His witnesses. It is little wonder that He commissioned *everyone* in the church—especially given the high price He paid that all humankind might be won for eternity. He wants *you*, my friend! This last instruction, His final commandment, is the greatest one: to witness to others. It is His heart's desire.

> Your love for Jesus should compel you to share that love with others!

You say you love God. You pray, attend church, and read the Bible. All of these are great things. Still, Jesus described what loving Him truly looks like when He said, "If you love Me, keep My commandments" (John 14:15). And I believe His final command is the most important! You see, salvation purchased by Jesus Christ is more than just "fire insurance" protecting us from hell. It is the start of a new life of purpose. That purpose is found in His last words in Acts—to tell others about Him.

Jesus has a marketing plan. And that plan is you and me! Jesus has no plan B, no contingency plan. He has left the responsibility of communicating His desire to save all of humanity, even the very gospel for which He came to earth and died, in the hands of Christians—everyday Christians like you and me. He plants us shoulder to shoulder with the people of the lost, workaday world, and He says to us, as He did to the disciples on that Mount of Ascension, "You shall be My witnesses." Jesus desire is that you would be a witness to your family, neighbors, friends, and coworkers where He has placed you.

How do you think the typical believer measures up in fulfillment of the Lord's last commandment before leaving the earth? Unfortunately, many of the Christians I've talked to say that they do not regularly share the gospel. It is perhaps unsurprising, although alarming, that a Pew poll indicates 72 percent of Americans believe religion is losing influence in our nation.[1] There are certainly a number of factors to blame, but more importantly, consider this: How are you doing in fulfilling the Great Commission in your life? Are you regularly sharing the good news of the gospel with your friends and family, neighbors and coworkers? Are you open about your faith?

> **Jesus has a marketing plan: you.**

Imagine if you took a show of hands next Sunday morning at your church of those who have led someone to Christ this year—or perhaps ever in their lives. It is not an exaggeration to guess that in any given American evangelical church, on any Sunday morning, few hands would go up. For most, witnessing is uncomfortable at best and almost counterintuitive to our postmodern lifestyle. It is as if there is some overarching rule that sharing spiritual things is an out-of-bounds subject or unnecessarily awkward. The advice of our unbiblical culture is "Don't bring up politics or religion." We easily buy it. I have!

Once, I was out to dinner with my daughter, Naomi. We were in a resort area, and it was late evening. As we left the dinner, there in the lot was this magnificent, lighted, white Cinderella-like horse-drawn carriage for rent for a short jaunt. I thought, *This would really make Naomi feel special*, so I rented it for a fifteen-minute ride. This entailed waiting about thirty minutes for the carriage to become available, and during this time I became engaged in conversation with the owner. Then I felt it... the nudge of the Holy Spirit.

> **How do you respond to the nudging of the Holy Spirit?**

You probably know the feeling well. It is that inner nudge, thought, or conviction to share about your faith. The situation with the friendly carriage owner was a perfect setup to inquire about his spiritual beliefs. But I wasn't sure how he might respond and honestly wasn't up to investing the time in such a conversation, so I ignored the nudge—I never mentioned Jesus to him. How do you respond to the nudging of the Holy Spirit? The truth is that our busy and increasingly impersonal lives (read: Facebook "friends") are somehow out of sync with the face-to-face, time-consuming interaction required to get to know someone long enough to truly impact them with your faith. Sharing Christ is a personal and deeply relational experience. Yet for most of us, it probably looks more like this: you find yourself in the presence of someone, whether a coworker, friend, acquaintance (carriage owner), or someone you just rub shoulders with. You suspect (or it is obvious) that this person is lost—not a believer. Though you might wonder about their faith, scarce is the Christian today who will muster up the courage to even risk a "God bless you" or put a tract in their hand, much less ask that person about his or her spiritual convictions. You're just uncomfortable with it.

Imagine for a moment if the opposite reality were true. What if each of us who love the Lord and sincerely follow Jesus would take up the task of leading just *one* person to Christ annually?

Friend, the truth is that if every Christ-follower (each of us) won one, the church would double in one year. Could this begin with you?

Herein lies the challenge of American Christianity. There are many things we *say* are the deeply held aspects of our faith in Jesus—things like tithing, prayer, and Bible reading. But who you are is, in reality, fully defined by what you *do*, not by what you *say* you do. Among these fondly confessed aspects of Christianity, witnessing to others is commonly the most neglected. Or to quote an anthropologist whom I recently read, "What people say, what people do, and what they say they do are entirely different things."[2]

> **If every Christ-follower would lead one person to Christ annually, the church would double in one year.**

This artificial contentment with the rhetorical instead of the actual is popular in our culture. We live in a sound-bite, virtually oriented society where we can post most anything on social media, which may or may not represent reality. We may send overly favorable selfies, drive a new car, live in a nice house with a large flatscreen TV, and look successful, yet be tens of thousands of dollars in debt beyond our ability to repay. Image can become more important than truth. We may say we want to share Christ—but we miss opportunities to do so. But the good news is, it is never too late to begin! To sum it all up:

- Sharing the gospel is Jesus greatest and last expressed desire.
- Your love for Jesus should birth in you an eagerness to share Him with others.

- We conceptually embrace the value of evangelism but rarely practice it.
- Christian society affirms beliefs in the absence of practicing them, just as our society embraces image over content.

Remember, the yardstick of your faith—the Word of God—reinforces the importance of Christ-centeredness in your life. It makes a powerful and all-encompassing statement about Jesus—that He is literally at the center of *everything*. Consider Ephesians 1:10, which says, "In the dispensation of the fullness of the times He might gather together *in one all things in Christ*, both which are in heaven and which are on earth—in Him" (emphasis mine). Check out the magnitude of this incredible statement! All of time (dispensation) and history (fullness of time) is gathered in this one person, Jesus. All things will ultimately find their nexus and purpose in Him. God is saying that the sum of *everything*—creation, humanity, the heavens—is found solely in Jesus Christ!

> **Who you are is fully defined by what you do, not by what you say you do.**

If only you could make this same claim in your life! To say that my work, entertainment, family, funds, and (perhaps most importantly) my delights all find their purpose and summation in Jesus Christ is the essence of overcoming. This is what Jesus deserves, because He is God and is worthy of nothing less! In other words, what Ephesians 1:10 says is that Jesus is God's master plan for all of creation and for your life.

Recently, I had breakfast with my accountability partner, Stan. I love this guy because he exemplifies what it looks like to have a preoccupation with Jesus. We were sharing our recent experiences with our families and our need as men to be there for our wives and kids. In that discussion, we came to the conclusion that both our wives share the same primary love language: quality time. Stan told me, "I love spending time with my wife, but there is always this burning desire deep within me to go out and win more for Jesus."

Like Stan, are you passionate about sharing your faith? This heart of preoccupation with the person of Jesus is biblical—look at the apostle Paul's words: "For to me, to live is Christ, and to die is gain" (Philippians 1:21). For Paul, life was all about Jesus Christ, and death was even better because Paul got to be with Him. In this statement, Paul mirrored the same views found in Ephesians 1:10 about Jesus being the summation of creation. Look at his clarity of focus on Jesus when he made the following statement in 1 Corinthians 9:16: "For if I preach the gospel, I have nothing to boast of, for necessity is laid upon me; yes, woe is me if I do not preach the gospel!" Here Paul, the man who wrote several books of the Bible, basically said he's toast if he doesn't preach the gospel!

> **Paul, the apostle of grace, was under compulsion to share the gospel.**

Does this mean that he was trying to earn his way to heaven? Absolutely not. Paul was the apostle of grace—the very author of the book of Romans, which speaks of salvation by grace through faith alone. Still, Paul himself stated that it doesn't *end* with grace; he was under compulsion to preach the gospel, which is the good news of Christ, and he was in desperate shape if he did not. The same applies to you! It is God's plan for you to share the gospel to bring kingdom increase. Yet, to quote my friend Dr. Tom Eads, "The quickest way to bring an awkward silence among a group of Christians is to talk about Jesus." And so, what should be central to your faith often goes overlooked or forgotten.

This is not to trap you in guilt or punishment, but rather to spur you to action. The gospel is good news that you get the privilege of sharing. Is your faith practical or rhetorical? I'm just saying, this is what the Word says—to be Jesus witnesses. If you are serious about being a *biblical* Christ-follower, how can you reconcile yourself to silence if the writer of the majority of the New Testament was under this compulsion to testify about and share Jesus message? How can we do less?

The challenge you face—the problem with twenty-first-century Christians—is that we repeat in our minds and with our lips this fondly held set of values we quietly refuse to *practice*. For example, we say we believe in tithing, but the average believer only gives 2.5 percent.[3] We say we believe in prayer, but do you spend regular, focused time each day with the Savior?

> Is your faith practical or rhetorical?

This is a weakness brought to you by our culture; we are a spectator society. We think that we are part of a team, when in fact we are only in the stands cheering instead of on the field, in exhaustion, actually playing the game. This should not be the case with our faith. We would be wise to follow Paul's example in perseverance and finish the race that God has set out for us (see 2 Timothy 4:7).

As a Christian, you are called to active participation in the outworking of your faith. Not only is this God's plan for you, but it brings heavenly rewards! Sharing your faith is a joy that many Christians today miss out on. Often our Christian practice stands in stark contrast to that of the apostle Paul who said, "Woe is me if I do not preach the gospel!" (1 Corinthians 9:16). Our aversion to witnessing may rather be characterized by reversing Paul's words and saying, "Woe is me if I have to share the gospel!" This spectator mentality is also displayed in the parable of the two sons found in Matthew 21:28–32.

> "But what do you think? A man had two sons, and he came to the first and said, 'Son, go, work today in my vineyard.' He answered and said, 'I will not,' but afterward he regretted it and went. Then he came to the second and said likewise. And he answered and said, 'I go, sir,' but he did not go. Which of the two did the will of his father?"
> They said to Him, "The first."
> Jesus said to them, "Assuredly, I say to you that tax collectors and harlots enter the kingdom of God before you. For John came to you in the way of righteousness, and you did not believe him; but tax collectors and harlots believed him; and when you saw it, you did not afterward relent and believe him."

Jesus was not speaking this parable to the "unchurched," if you will, of His day. Rather, He was saying this to the people of God—in fact, the leaders of His kingdom on earth at the time: Israel. The essence of what Jesus conveyed through this story is simply this: it pleases God when you actually *do* His will. What Jesus really cares about, according to the parable, is your actions rather than your words. No matter how much you study the Bible, agree with the ideas, and accept God's will, remaining idle is not actually implementing the Father's purpose. It is worth a reminder that Jesus told parables not only for those who were listening then, but also as a record for us as today's church.

The parable of the two sons is a call to action and an

indictment against lip service. We find this concept addressed again in the book of James where we are told to "be *doers of the word*, and not hearers only, deceiving yourselves" (1:22, emphasis mine). You are called to *do* amazing things for Jesus! It says in 1 Corinthians 10:11, "Now all these things happened to them as examples, and they were written for our admonition, upon whom the ends of the ages have come"—that, friend, is you and I, the latest generation of believers on earth.

> **We believe church attendance, Bible reading, and prayer fulfill our purpose as Christ-followers . . . but there is more!**

Could this parable be applied to evangelicals today? One morning, when I was leading the prayer time with the staff of a national ministry, I posed the question: If you attend Sunday church, midweek group, study the Bible, love God, pray daily, tithe, and live holy . . . are you fully doing God's will on earth? The participants eagerly agreed that yes, you would be. Not a single person caught the elephant in the room, the greatest purpose for your salvation and life—witnessing!

We believe church attendance, Bible reading, and prayer fulfill our purpose as faithful Christ-followers . . . but there is more! These things are important for sure. Yet it is worth asking, how are you *applying God's Word* in your giving, praying, and especially in the area of evangelism? Are you being faithful? Like the first son in the parable, you *say* you will be . . . but you may not always act accordingly. Most Christians believe in the importance of these things, yet do you have the will to act on what you believe? Your walk with the Lord is meant to be more than *words* and mental accession to a set of truths. God's Word echoes the value of acting on faith in Philippians 2:13, which says, "It is God who works in you both to will and to do for His good pleasure." Thankfully, you are never alone in your efforts.

Working Together with the Spirit of God

Applying your faith to share with others can be the most interesting and fulfilling aspect of your daily life if you allow God to guide you. Each day you are capable of being led by the Holy Spirit to labor with Him to *change hearts*. He is doing the work—after all, you certainly don't have the power to change anyone! Yet God chooses you to be a vessel to carry His transforming message: "But we have this treasure in earthen vessels, that the excellence of the power may be of God and not of us" (2 Corinthians 4:7). This is what is meant by working together with Him. Paul brought truth; the Holy Spirit brought healing. Paul brought teaching; the Holy Spirit brought conviction. This is the great adventure of the Christian life! Friend, God is ready to use you in mighty ways and bless you beyond measure into eternity.

> **Your walk with the Lord is meant to be more than words and mental accession to a set of truths.**

Your walk with the Lord is intended to be an intimate fellowship. Your being led by the Holy Spirit, together *demonstrating* works destined to bring increase and fulfill God's kingdom purposes while on earth, is thankfully not done of your own accord. It is only through the power of the Spirit that others will be drawn to Jesus. We see this in 1 Corinthians 2:4, which affirms, "My speech and my preaching were not with persuasive words of human wisdom, but in demonstration of the Spirit and of power." The Holy Spirit is your "intimate Ally" as you walk through the daily experiences of life. This is why the Spirit was sent to believers. When Jesus was on the earth, He clearly demonstrated the validity of His divinity and message by performing works of power to change people's lives. Then He said He was going to send His replacement: "Nevertheless I tell you the truth. It is to your advantage that I go away; for if I do not go away, the Helper will not come to you; but if I depart, I will send Him to you" (John 16:7).

Jesus is saying here that it's to His advantage and our advantage that the Holy Spirit comes. Because Jesus sent His Helper, we have access to God's power 24-7! The Spirit provides Jesus' personal understanding, power, and love in each situation we encounter. The Holy Spirit is Jesus' replacement on earth, while Jesus is at the right hand of God in heaven interceding for us—which is His next great ministry after achieving the ministry of redemption. Sending the Holy Spirit to believers is Jesus' great plan to expand His church. While Jesus was on earth and in a physical body, He was only one man and could only do so much because He chose to take on human limitations. For instance, He could not be everywhere all at once. But when He sent the Holy Spirit to live in each one of us, our Lord's power and presence expanded dramatically through each of us! As a believer, you have the Holy Spirit interceding on your behalf to Almighty God!

Who is the Holy Spirit? John 16:7 uses a term *paraklétos*, which translates to "comforter." In the New Testament's original language of Koine Greek, the word *paraklétos* (παράκλητος) means "one who is beside you to counsel you."[4] What is the role and counsel of the Holy Spirit in coming to dwell within you? Scripture gives the answer in the next verse: "And when He has come, He will convict the world of sin, and of righteousness, and of judgment" (John 16:8). This is a comforting thought—that it is not your job to bring conviction when sharing your faith in Jesus Christ. All you are is a vessel to impart, in a loving and winsome way, the truth. Then it is up to God to bring increase, to bring conviction, to help people feel that the gospel message is relevant to their lives. You can't do that part of the process; only God can.

Recently I had the great privilege of talking with my eighteen-year-old college freshman grandson. Everyone else had gone to bed, and we were in the kitchen discussing his life and his new college career. Then I shared with him an illustration about how the way you live in the short span of earthly existence determines your destination in eternity. I asked him if he knew for sure whether he would go to heaven if he died tomorrow. He said, "Well, I think I'm a good enough person that I would."

Engaging him further, I asked, "So have you ever told a lie?"

He conceded that he had. I continued, "Have you ever had a wrong thought about a woman?"

He replied, "Yes, I have."

I said, "That's called sin . . . so does that make you a 'good person'?"

He acknowledged that my point was valid. I then went through the Romans Road[5] and shared with him the gospel of Jesus Christ. I told him the truth about how he could find eternal life in the work of the cross and how he could get to heaven.

I did what I could in imparting the gospel to him—but it wasn't enough. It was time to ask for a commitment. At this point, I realized my total inadequacy to do anything but speak the truth—God had to finish the work. Only God could

> **I realized my inadequacy to do anything but speak the truth—God had to finish the work.**

convict his heart. Only God could show him that committing to Christ was important enough for him to do—that he felt the need for it.

So I simply asked, "Is this free gift of eternal life something you would like to receive?"

He replied, "Yes, it is."

It was obvious that he was under conviction. I said, "Would you like to pray right now to receive Jesus Christ as your Savior?" Thankfully he did! We prayed a teary-eyed and heartfelt prayer together, with my leading and him receiving in his own words Christ as his Lord and Savior! This is a perfect example of our limitations; I spoke the truth, but only God could enter into his heart and give him a longing and a felt need for acting on it.

In each conversation, with each person you meet, the Holy Spirit can provide empowering insight and impart the gospel's relevance to that person's mind and heart. I believe this is what the apostle Peter meant when he said in 2 Peter 1:3, "His divine power has given to us all things that pertain to life and godliness, through the knowledge of Him who called us by glory and virtue." The Spirit of God gives you and me the power to be effective witnesses.

When we talk about the power of the Holy Spirit in church culture (particularly in charismatic circles), it is often portrayed as "signs" (i.e., the working of miracles, healings, being slain in the Spirit, speaking in tongues). I do not think that is what Peter meant in the previous verse. The Holy Spirit's work is much more than that. The purpose of the Holy Spirit is not signs and wonders; it is to glorify Jesus. It's being able to see the ways that God brings about circumstances and shows the relevance of the gospel—in revealing true knowledge of Him—to the heart of each person you run into. Let's examine what Jesus said about the work of the Spirit: "However, when

He, the Spirit of truth, has come, He will guide you into all truth; for He will not speak on His own authority, but whatever He hears He will speak; and He will tell you things to come. *He will glorify Me*, for He will take of what is Mine and declare it to you" (John 16:13–14, emphasis mine).

The Holy Spirit will guide you in what to say in each circumstance—and the main message the Spirit brings every time is to glorify Jesus! The biblical manifestation of the Holy Spirit's work in your life is not restricted to signs and wonders. The purpose of the Spirit of God, according to Jesus, is to lead you into truth, which will bring glory to Christ and blessing to you. This is to be the essence of your Christianity.

> **The purpose of the Holy Spirit is not signs and wonders; it is to testify of and glorify Jesus.**

Second Timothy 3:5 is convicting when it says "having a form of godliness but denying its power." Isn't this what "religion" is—a set of man-made beliefs devoid of the living God? Not so with your faith! Jesus Christ is alive in you and me, through His Holy Spirit. This Comforter validates the biblical truths that we hold so dear, by the demonstration of His love, kindness, care, and conviction for us and for those we meet and share the good news with. It is this very practical, real hourly concept of the Holy Spirit in us that motivated the apostle Paul to make the following statement: "For we are God's fellow workers; you are God's field, you are God's building" (1 Corinthians 3:9). In this verse are a few exciting truths. The first is that God *wants* you to labor, as we've already seen.

Second, He doesn't leave you alone to do the work—He wants to be involved. You have the incredible privilege of actually working together with the God of heaven—"Christ in you" (Colossians 1:27) through the Holy Spirit. Being used by the Holy Spirit to speak of Jesus is the greatest purpose of the believer and the greatest desire of Jesus Himself for you and me. In so doing, we glorify Jesus with our lives.

Heaven's rewards and our ability in overcoming in order to receive them are inextricably tied to the word of our testimony. The Holy Spirit in us makes this powerful and easy. In the next chapter, we'll take a closer look at what sharing the gospel is, conversely what it is not, and why this is so important to our Father.

TIME	TO	GATE	REMARK
10:00	HEAVEN	A10	DELAYED
10:02	HEAVEN	A03	ON-TIME
10:08	HEAVEN	A06	CANCELED
10:09	HEAVEN	A12	ON-TIME
10:12	HEAVEN	B07	ON-TIME
10:14	HEAVEN	B02	DELAYED
10:21	HEAVEN	H07	ON-TIME

This Is Your Captain Speaking

Whenever I'm on a flight and the captain makes an announcement, I pay attention. After all, wouldn't I want to listen to the pilot who is keeping the plane in the air and on course? There are certain times when someone's words matter more. In the same way that I tune in to the captain's and flight crew's instructions, you are called to tune in to the purposes of God. He is your guide through turbulent times, and He is always directing your path. It is never too late to listen for His still small voice.

Do you remember the businessman from chapter 5? We were seated beside each other, engaged in spiritual conversation. The man was receptive and admitted that he'd recently been considering matters of eternity. The opportunity presented itself for me to share my beliefs and the message of the cross, and I was faithful to share. I could have left the discussion there and turned back to my own interests. I could have read a book or gotten some work done. That would have been the more comfortable option.

But then, I felt it . . . the pressure, that nudge. I had shared the gospel. I had spoken truth to him, and now came the time when an invitation should be given. But we were sitting on an airplane. There were people to my right. It was not an ideal setting for an intimate commitment! Yet I felt God's conviction, so I asked him, "After all that you've heard, do you feel like God is moving your heart to give your life to Jesus Christ right now? Would you like to make that commitment?" He paused for a moment as tears welled up in his eyes. Then he said, in a very heartfelt voice, "I sure would." He prayed to receive Jesus as his Lord and Savior, right there on the plane.

Your words are a way for the Holy Spirit to accomplish the purposes of God. This middle-aged businessman was clearly mulling over eternity in his mind long before I met him. Yet the Holy Spirit, who is Lord, knew his heart and how to touch him intimately. A man found eternal life when words spoken in faith reached him with the gospel message. You can be encouraged that the Holy Spirit is at work in you and through you to bring people to salvation as well.

What Will You Do to Have Your Best Life in Eternity?

1. Recall the most important words you have ever spoken or that were spoken to you. Why were they so impactful?

2. Do you agree that Jesus last words on earth for you to be His witness was a deep expression of His heart? Why or why not?

3. When you feel the nudge of the Holy Spirit, how do you respond? Do you behave more like the first son (action) or the second son (words) from Jesus parable?

4. Have you thought of the Holy Spirit's purpose being to help testify about Jesus rather than provide signs? How can this enhance your confidence in testifying?

5. Take inventory of your obedience to the Great Commission. When was the last time you told somebody about Jesus? What are some of the obstacles to sharing your faith?

6. Who are the hardest and easiest people to talk to about Jesus? What could you do to make witnessing an easier task? When will you start?

Chapter Seven
Avoiding the Trap

That I may open my mouth boldly to make known the mystery of the gospel.
—*Ephesians 6:19*

We have written about sharing our faith. To offer a clearer understanding of what it means to testify to your faith, let me share a story of my encounter with another passenger during my travels. After I had taken my seat on the plane, I took note of the man sitting next to me. His first-class seat, luxury watch, and custom suit revealed that this man was well off and likely an executive of some sort. (As an aside, I have concluded that first-class air is generally for two kinds of people: those with enough disposable cash to spend on it or unfortunate sorts like myself who have accumulated so many air miles that they get an upgrade!) In any case, I was interested to find out more about my amiable fellow passenger.

I shot up a quick prayer asking the Lord if He had anything He wanted me to say to the man. As with the businessman I mentioned in chapter 5, the following verse came to mind: "What will it profit a man if he gains the whole world, and loses his own soul?" (Mark 8:36). After approximately forty-five minutes of connecting with the guy (and finding out that he had two homes in London, one in Manhattan, and one in Naples), he commented, "You know, I really need to spend more of my savings soon. Who knows how much longer I'll be around to use it?" (He was in his late sixties.) Now *that* was a softball, an opening—thank you, Jesus—and I mentioned the verse. As with the first businessman, he had considered matters of eternity and was open to talking with me further, which began an engaging discussion on spiritual beliefs. My seatmate revealed himself to be a studied atheist who approached the world through logic. A slave to his own rationality, he was interested in the afterlife, examined it, and came up dry because it could not be empirically proven. His sad conclusion was that "we're no different from animals after we die," which I thought was rather demeaning and depressing, standing in stark contrast to his apparent opulent lifestyle.

I thanked him for opening up and sharing his perspective with me. Then I asked if he'd like to hear my thoughts on the subject. He agreed, so I explained my beliefs, and then I used my favorite reasoning for conversing with an atheist. I told him, "If you are right and there is no afterlife, we both will end up the same." He readily agreed that this was so. "But," I said, "if I am right and there is a God, then you are in deep water!" With a business-oriented spin, I encouraged him to cover his eternal "downside risk," and I shared the gospel with him.

Clarity of the Gospel Shared

The word *gospel* literally means "good news"[1]—and it very much is. Though Ponce de León never found the storied fountain of youth, and no amount of antiaging cosmetics, plastic surgeries, or dietary regimens will stave off death, the gospel is the true wellspring of eternal life. The gospel simply promises you will live forever (see John 8:51) in paradise (heaven) with God. *But* it is conditional upon affirming and believing certain truths. Sharing the gospel is foundational to bringing increase and hearing Jesus tell you, "Well done." Here is a simple way to remember it.

The Three S's

SIN—I conveyed to my newfound atheist friend that God does not want any of us to perish. However, to live forever in the presence of a holy God, you have a problem—your *sinfulness*. At this point, I asked my seatmate whether he had ever sinned; he was honest in confessing that he had. I shared that all of us have sinned and fallen short of God's perfect standard of holiness (see Romans 3:23), and without righteousness none of us would see Him. That presents a problem you cannot solve yourself.

SOLUTION—The problem is that your sin keeps you from experiencing life with a holy God—but there is good news! I shared that God has provided a *solution*. While you were yet in opposition to God, Christ died for you. The just died for the unjust, bringing you into companionship with Him (see 1 Peter 3:18). The righteous dying for the unrighteous, God dying for man. He took your punishment, paying your penalty. I asked the man beside me if he believed this in his heart.

SALVATION—At this point, my acquaintance had heard the gospel but had not affirmed his faith in the message. He had not accepted it as his own. The Word says, "If you *confess* with your mouth the Lord Jesus and *believe* in your heart that God has raised Him from the dead, you will be saved" (Romans 10:9, emphasis mine). You

> **Confession precedes conversion.**

see, "out . . . of the heart the mouth speaks" (Matthew 12:34). Jesus practiced this when He asked the blind man, "Do you believe I can make you see?" (Matthew 9:28 NLT). You speak what is in your heart, what you believe. Confession precedes conversion. The gospel is incomplete without a "call to action" ... an *invitation*.

Just as we know that faith without works is dead, so, too, we know that Jesus calls us to a life of acting on belief in the gospel. It is not enough to know the truth; you must act on it by surrendering your life to Christ. James stated that the devil himself believes ... but is not born again (see James 2:19). He has not volitionally placed his eternal destiny in Jesus hands; he does not have saving faith. In contrast, when you perform good works in Jesus name, you reveal the heart change that has taken place in you. Friend, you are being transformed from the inside out by the power of the gospel!

Ultimately, the plan for sharing the good news is simple. A problem of sin, a solution—Christ's sacrifice, and an offer to receive this salvation by faith. All three components make up the fullness of the gospel of Jesus Christ. All are necessary for an unbeliever to receive the free gift of eternal life. When you combine these truths and share them clearly, God works on the hearts of those around you, and you are able to bring increase to the kingdom.

The Rest of the Story

I take this reality to heart, so after explaining the problem and solution of the human condition, I invited my new atheist friend to personally place his faith in Christ. I asked him whether he believed the message of the cross and was ready to take a step of faith. It may surprise you to hear that he outright declined! Although I believe it was evident that my acquaintance was under conviction, he was an empirically based rationalist who was unwilling to embrace the gospel message as truth. He had *heard* a clear presentation of the good news, but he was unsaved because he declined the opportunity to receive it as his own.

Interestingly, something very unusual happened directly after our conversation. It was late at night, and we were about 37,000 feet in the air. My new friend had the window seat. After he declined the invitation to accept Christ, we amicably chatted a bit until he glanced out the window. It just happened to be the time of year when one of the planets was closest in orbit to the Earth, and it was clear he had never seen this sight before. At 37,000 feet the celestial anomaly looked gargantuan. I watched as his refined composure quickly melted into a momentary look of terror as he asked, "What in the world is that?" with obvious distress. For an instant, my seatmate was faced with the terror of his own mortality in the face of something that he thought was outside of his rationality. A hardened, empirically oriented, self-proclaimed atheist . . . terrified. I assured him that it was just a season of the year for the planet to be that close. However, in that moment I caught a glimpse of the hopelessness underlying the thin veneer of atheism. A fitting capstone to the gospel discussion, I thought.

> **A hardened, empirically oriented, self-proclaimed atheist . . . terrified.**

While I can venture a guess as to why the first businessman (chapter 5) was more receptive to the gospel message than the second, I may never know for sure why one reached the point of conversion during our conversation while the other did not. Thankfully, it's not up to me to control the other person's response. Our responsibility, yours and mine, is simply to share the gospel faithfully and clearly to the best of our ability. And we are greatly rewarded when we do! The aim of this chapter is to give you tools to do just that. Now that I have shared a simple outline of what the gospel is, let's take a look at some of the things commonly mistaken as "sharing the gospel." What you may realize is that some of the concepts that we glibly accept as sharing the gospel are actually a veiled trap to avoid doing so.

What Gospel Sharing Is Not
Your Testimony

I fondly remember, years ago, going door-to-door each Wednesday night with Evangelism Explosion[2] through my church. We spoke to dozens of families in our small town. EE has a great formula that includes sharing your testimony of what Christ has done for you personally. But wisely, it does not leave the conversation there. One of the final steps is a call to action. EE and other evangelism methods are good but often require memorizing or following a script, which can sound a bit rehearsed amid the spontaneity of personal witness. Still, it is a useful tool to begin witnessing with a framework in mind, so that you are prepared to give an answer for the hope that you have (see 1 Peter 3:15). We will closely examine some of these methods in chapter 9.

> Your testimony is a great springboard for sharing the gospel.

When witnessing, using your testimony as a starting point is beneficial, credible, and nearly irrefutable. Speaking about the ways that committing to Jesus has changed your life provides a great springboard to ask folks if they want to do the same and for sharing the gospel. The important thing, though, is to bring it home—others need to know that they, too, can place their faith in the living Christ. They need to be *asked*. A testimony without a gospel invitation is incomplete. Sharing your salvation experience is useful as an example of how and why to come to faith in Christ. However, it is not necessarily the same as sharing the gospel. Without an invitation and a call to action, your testimony is only a (compelling) personal story. There is more that is necessary in order to be faithful to bring increase and hear the words "well done."

Let's return to the airplane where we left the atheist businessman who refused my invitation. I had presented his need to dispose of his sin through Christ's sacrifice. Though he rejected this, he appeared to be under conviction. At this point, I told him some of the supernatural things God has done in my life. While he did not reach a moment of conversion during our conversation, this personal testimony from a credible source (he had not written me off as a religious nut because I had first gotten to know him and engaged him in conversation) had an impact on him. I could tell that God was working on his heart and used our interaction as part of the process. My new friend invited me to stay in touch. My testimony provided a way for me to share my faith and a gospel invitation. You can use your story to share the gospel and invite others to Christ too!

The Silent Witness—"I Just Want to Show Them the Gospel"

Perhaps, rather than forgetting to include an invitation after sharing your testimony, you instead struggle with sharing about Jesus in the first place. I remember visiting a pregnancy center in the Deep South during one of my ministry trips. Their mission statement demonstrated a desire to see the women who visited this ministry come to know Jesus as Lord. As the leader of the center and I spoke, she passionately expressed their desire to show the love of Christ through acts of compassion and benevolence. The organization would meet the women's needs emotionally in the middle of unplanned pregnancy and provide physical necessities like diapers, clothing, etc. They did an excellent job of loving their clients. This love was a clear demonstration of God's love to the women they served. But when I inquired about how many of the women actually came to a saving faith in Christ, she knew of very few.

Although the team loved the women sacrificially in a multitude of ways, her center's end goal was not currently being met—only a scarce number of the women God sent actually received the gift of eternal life. Many received maternity clothes and emotional support, but few received salvation. What was happening?

> **The silent witness is a cultural appeasement for believers not to share Jesus at all.**

The answer is that the center was lacking *balance*. There must be a balance of love and truth in the Christian life. We see this emulated most clearly in Jesus Christ's character. Remember how He was, very early in the gospel of John, described: "We beheld His glory, the glory as of the only begotten of the Father, full of *grace* and *truth*" (John 1:14, emphasis mine). In Jesus we see the balance. He is full of grace—the mercy of God expressed without your merit. Jesus was the embodied characterization of perfect balance. He loved the sinner and chided the Pharisee. He fed the thousands, but He then taught them. He held His tongue with Pilate and ran out the money changers who were desecrating the temple. He healed with compassion and taught with truth. Balance is a rare thing, but it is necessary in order to be like Christ. Love without truth can be sentimentalism; truth without love can be harsh. And the silent witness is a cultural appeasement for believers not to share Jesus at all. You must love and speak truth—both.

The women working at this pregnancy center were experts in the love aspect of Christ's character. They were mercy-gifted grace givers to women in many outward expressions of faith. It's true that Jesus new command was exactly this—to love one another and thus fulfill the law of Christ. He even said this would be a distinctive characteristic of His followers: "A new commandment I give to you, that you love one another; as I have loved you, that you also love one another" (John 13:34). This is a blessed and joyful privilege for you to live out. God is pleased with you when people readily observe the difference in your life by the love you show. "May the Lord make you increase and abound in love to one another and to all, just as we do to you" (1 Thessalonians 3:12). Supernatural love and concern for the weak is certainly a hallmark of your faith and thankfully separates you from the religions of the world. It is how your faith is lived out. To love your enemies and bless those who curse you is proof that you and I are different from the world. While that love is not verbally communicating the gospel, it certainly validates it.

If you attribute only your loving actions to communicating your faith, it is not the complete gospel message. While it is a good thing, offering acts of social justice and mercy to the lost is actually not the best way to love them. Is it really loving another well to clothe, feed, counsel, house, or provide for them and then neglect to share the truth of how they can spend eternity with God? Yes, these acts are imperative, but they are temporary. They are your calling card—your credibility—for the gospel, offering another the fulfillment of their greatest need: salvation through faith in Christ. That salvation comes only

> **Your acts of mercy are the calling card for the gospel.**

through imparting the truth of the life, death, and resurrection of Jesus. When it came to the balance of truth, few of the pregnancy care workers presented the gospel, so of the women in their care, only a few came to confess Jesus as Lord. They prioritized action without words.

You may have heard it said—and maybe spoken it yourself—"I want to show the gospel by my actions" or "I want to live out the gospel in front of them," or perhaps you've heard the phrase "lifestyle evangelism." All of these are good things, as you should live a life that complements your witness. The old adage holds true here, though—often the good can be the enemy of the best. Let's unpack this together.

First, it is a good thing to live a life that complements the gospel. A good reputation and a lifestyle witness before the Lord are important to not compromising—or even contradicting—the message of Jesus Christ. I am all for living in such a manner that "adorns" the gospel of the Lord. This is thoroughly biblical too:

> In all things showing yourself to be a pattern of good works; in doctrine showing integrity, reverence, incorruptibility, sound speech that cannot be condemned, that one who is an opponent may be ashamed, having nothing evil to say of you. Exhort bondservants to be obedient to their own masters, to be well pleasing in all things, not answering back, not pilfering, but showing all good fidelity, that they may adorn the doctrine of God our Savior in all things. (Titus 2:7–10)

God Himself instructs us to live a holy life: "As He who called you is holy, you also be holy in all your conduct, because it is written, 'Be holy, for I am holy'" (1 Peter 1:15–16). Witnessing must go beyond lifestyle, however. A silent witness, though important in itself, is insufficient to bring salvation to anyone. It is wishful thinking to hope that observing our acts of love or social justice will bring another to conviction and repentance. I have been living for Jesus for thirty years, and not one time in that span has anyone come up to me and said, "There's something different about you. Tell me about what you have that I don't."

Now, I hope it is not because I have a poor silent witness—I believe I am living a joy-filled and obedient Christian walk. I worked for decades surrounded by unsaved people in the transportation industry at a trucking company—not exactly a bastion of holiness! Amid this, my coworkers knew I was different and a Christ-follower. From time to time they would (usually in confidence) come to me in private with a problem or seeking counsel. Yet this generally did not result in them getting saved or wanting to "have what I have." Living faithfully requires words along with actions.

Still, isn't there a popular saying, "Preach the gospel at all times, if necessary use words"? The idea here is that somehow a Christ-centered life would clearly communicate the plan of salvation and invite others to Jesus. This is hopeful, yet misguided. It is the opposite of the Word of God, which says, "So then faith comes by hearing, and hearing by the word of God" (Romans 10:17). In Acts 4:20 the disciples said, "We cannot but speak of the things which we have seen and heard." Somehow in modern Christian culture we have confused showing the love of Christ with sharing the gospel of Christ. They are distinct from one another. Faith in Jesus comes by hearing about and understanding His sacrifice on the cross—by hearing the truth of His life, death, and resurrection, not just observing good works done by His

> "We cannot but speak the things which we have seen and heard." (Acts 4:20)

followers (you and me). Many faiths encourage good works, but it is the truthful sharing of Christ's work—God becoming man—that distinguishes the gospel.

While it is good to show the love of God as an expression of the gospel, the Bible says in Romans 10:17 that faith comes through *hearing* the Word of God. If you expect to see those around you saved, you must *speak* the truth to them. It is not enough to simply model God's love—as good as this is. You must *share* the truth that will set them free. First Thessalonians 2:4 expresses this beautifully: "But as we have been approved by God to be entrusted with the gospel, even so we speak, not as pleasing men, but God who tests our hearts." This verse is a masterpiece, a road map for testifying about Jesus. Let's look at it closer.

"as we have been approved by God"
I am sure glad God has approved me! What a statement. God has approved each of us *for a purpose, an entrustment*. Friend, that means you! Your salvation is (or should be) your most treasured possession. If you had an endless supply of money, would you feel compelled to share it with others? This is the truth of your approval by God—His love is higher than the heavens are above the earth; it's endless. How can we rest content with our "eternal life insurance" to simply say "I'm good" and be unconcerned about sharing it with others? There is a better way, and it brings blessing!

"to be entrusted with the gospel"
What if you knew that everyone in the world—everyone—had a fatal disease. What if you had an endless supply of the remedy, a medicine or pill that would cure the disease if only they took it? Would you feel compelled to share the medicine, or would

you rest content to be cured yourself? I believe most of us would spend our lives pressing the pill into people's hands—convincing them of the deadly nature of their disease, the effectiveness of the remedy, and that they need to take the medicine.

You have been entrusted with such a remedy—it is the gospel! The disease is sin—worse than any earthly disease; it is eternally fatal. The gospel is your cure. It is everlasting and powerful. And you have an endless supply of it!

God speaks often of this sacred trust of gospel truth He has given you: "According to the glorious gospel of the blessed God which was committed to my trust" (1 Timothy 1:11). This concept of stewardship or entrustment is found in the context of hearing "well done" in the parable of the talents: "For it is just like a man about to go on a journey. He called his own servants and *entrusted* his possessions to them" (Matthew 25:14 CSB, emphasis mine). It is God's incredible gift to you!

"even so we speak"

In order for someone to receive Jesus as their Lord and Savior, they must have understanding of the truth of redemption; therefore, it must come through *words*. The gospel must be conveyed either in writing or by speaking.

It is clear from Scripture that faith comes through words. We've already seen this concept in Romans 10:17, which tells us, "So then faith comes by hearing, and hearing by the word of God." Galatians 3:2 again shows it is by hearing God's Word: "This only I want to learn from you: Did you receive the Spirit by the works of the law,

> **You have a choice—risk offending others to please God or live to please men.**

or by the hearing of faith?" This is really the beauty of God's Word—it does *not* depend on you! If you share the truth, it is the truth that will set them free! What a relief to know that the Word of God and the Spirit of God are responsible to do the convicting and heart changing—*not* you and me! This is why the verse says "so we speak," because we must *tell* others about Jesus. But so often we do not. The next part of the verse tells why we often struggle.

"not as pleasing men"
It is far easier to tiptoe around the topic of faith than to bring it up in conversation. The world has constructed warning signs against us sharing—here is one them: "Never talk about politics or religion." The presumption is that we will offend someone or get into an argument if we do. I believe one of the major hindrances to sharing Jesus is the desire to be people pleasers. We simply do not want to get involved deep enough to deal with the potential of an argument. We can fear the face of men. While we will deal with the fear factor shortly in the following chapter, it is worthwhile to note here that we must honestly assess whether we are more concerned about pleasing others than we are concerned about their eternal destiny.

You have a choice: risk offending others to please God or live to please men. While you certainly do not want to be offensive to those around you, God is ultimately the One you must please. You don't need to worry what others will think of you, because God is the One who determines your destiny and gives you abundant life!

There might be an exception when you're trying to lead a relative or someone you are regularly with in your life to Christ. In this case, careful attention must be paid to your witness. If your witness confirms your testimony, it is powerful.

"but God who tests our hearts"

The Lord searches the earth for those whose hearts belong to Him so that He can strengthen them (see 2 Chronicles 16:9). God is watching and seeks to reward the obedient. The verse contrasts this with pleasing men. Honestly, I have witnessed to many people every year. To my knowledge, there has never been a situation where it has offended any of those I spoke with. I winsomely speak the truth in love and concern for their eternal destiny, which I can impact through the truth of God's Word. The verse we've studied in 1 Thessalonians ends by revealing that God is examining our hearts in this matter. He is looking at our actions and motivations. He wants to see us living faithfully, because He desires for us to succeed in bringing kingdom increase. He sends people across our paths—it is not simply by chance but purposeful. He longs for their salvation; He died for them. He is watching what we will do: lovingly speak the truth that will secure their eternal life or let them slip away into eternity without offering the remedy of Jesus. Let's take another look at the complete verse: "But as we have been approved by God to be entrusted with the gospel, even so we speak, not as pleasing men, but God who tests our hearts" (1 Thessalonians 2:4).

> **Break with the self-obsessed pattern of American life and share Jesus!**

We see from this marvelous verse the importance of and pattern for sharing the good news about Jesus, and that it must be conveyed with words. However, this is not the usual course of our lives. It is sadly the exception, not the norm, that someone cares enough to take the time to share the vital truth of the cross. It is difficult but vital to break with the self-obsessed pattern of

American life and share Jesus! Here lies another misconception of the gospel.

Inviting Them to Church

Bringing someone to church is a wonderful segue to presenting the gospel. It is a good, important, and natural outgrowth of your faith to invite others to attend your church. You should do this as often as you can. But inviting someone to church is not the same as witnessing for Jesus; it is not sharing the gospel. Inviting your neighbor or friend to church can be a conversation starter to sharing the truth of Jesus Christ and hopefully will expose them (in most evangelical churches) to a presentation of the gospel. In this way, the goal of presenting the gospel is met.

But the "means" matters! Inviting another to church is a "safer" way to share the gospel, in a sense. It takes the responsibility—and the risk—off you. Yet the most effective invitation to accept Jesus is always the most personal one. If your heart is to see your loved one or friend saved, you should be willing and eager to ask them personally if they want to receive Christ's gift. You are the one who has the closer relationship with the party in question; you should be the one sharing. It is easy to invite the other person to church as a way to get off the hook of sharing the gospel personally, but the most loving, effective way to share Jesus is one-on-one. But by all means, invite others to church and use it as an entryway for the gospel! You have the potential to bring kingdom increase when you do.

Earth's Greatest Privilege

You have the incredible, joyful honor to introduce friends, loved ones, and acquaintances to the God of the universe. You and I hold the key to eternal life (the gospel) and know the path and the doorway to heaven. Jesus said, "I am the way, the truth, and the life" (John 14:6). The exclusive privilege of the Christian is to see a person transformed—born again—right before you. There are few things more exciting!

Others in the Bible knew this and serve as examples of this truth. The apostle Paul was deeply committed to sharing the gospel. Look what he wrote to the church in Corinth: "For if I preach the gospel, I have nothing to boast of, for necessity is laid upon me; yes, woe is me if I do not preach the gospel!" (1 Corinthians 9:16). Clearly the gospel was Paul's passion and mandate. It was the purpose of his life. But not only Paul's life—yours too. In fact, God brought you to Himself for the purpose of making you a minister of the gospel: "Now all things are of God, who has reconciled us to Himself through Jesus Christ, and has given us the ministry of reconciliation" (2 Corinthians 5:18).

Your first ministry is to love the Lord with all your heart, mind, soul, and strength. He gave you a heart to do so, by reconciling you to Himself. Your second ministry is to love your neighbor as yourself. That is the ministry of reconciliation given to each of us. You and I are ambassadors of the country of heaven. God has sent you into the world to recruit citizens for eternity. You have the incredible capacity to be used by God to change the eternal fate of those you meet who are unsaved. In fact, God is sending unbelievers into your life every day for this very reason: "We are ambassadors for Christ, as though God were pleading through us: we implore you on Christ's behalf, be reconciled to God" (2 Corinthians 5:20).

Even more exciting, you are a priest of God's holy nation. When you were born again, you were ordained as a minister, a priest of the gospel. Yes, *you*! First Peter 2:9 tells us, "But you are a chosen generation, a royal priesthood, a holy nation, His own special people, that you may proclaim the praises of Him who called you out of darkness into His marvelous light." God made you for this, which means you cannot fail! The worst thing that could happen in inviting people to eternity with Jesus is that they decline. Even then, they have heard the life-giving truth. The seed has been sown, and God may have another person harvest. Your efforts to share Jesus are never in vain, never without purpose or fruit. The Word of God never fails. Friend, you can be empowered to share your faith! You will be greatly blessed for it in eternity.

Sharing your faith is, in fact, the norm of a well-lived relationship with Christ. So why do you wait? What are the obstacles that prevent you from this delightful duty of sharing the gospel? I was personally surprised how many well-accepted ideas in Christian culture actually do prevent sharing! The good news is that you can overcome when you recognize what is holding you back. You, personally, can have a greater impact for Christ! We will take a closer look at a few of these hindrances in the following chapter.

TIME	TO	GATE	REMARK
10:00	HEAVEN	A10	DELAYED
10:02	HEAVEN	A03	ON-TIME
10:08	HEAVEN	A06	CANCELED
10:09	HEAVEN	A12	ON-TIME
10:12	HEAVEN	B07	ON-TIME
10:14	HEAVEN	B02	DELAYED
10:21	HEAVEN	H07	ON-TIME

Airplane Mode

One of the mild inconveniences of being on a plane is not being able to use your phone in the same way that you do on land. The "airplane mode" exists for this occasion, to turn off your Wi-Fi and data to avoid interference. It can certainly be frustrating to have limited communication. Still, I'm grateful that the protection is in place and that my signal won't interfere with the various sensors and equipment required to keep us in the air!

Sometimes, in the busyness of life, I wish there was a setting I could adjust to turn off the noise and be able to focus on what matters. Thankfully, God's signal is never jammed, and you always have access to communicate with Him.

I went out early one morning in Washington, DC to find a cup of coffee for Valerie, my wife. I had a busy day ahead of me, and I was admittedly distracted as I walked up to the 7-Eleven store. There I noticed a homeless man sitting on the sidewalk beside the door. He looked like he had been there all night, or maybe more. I felt the conviction to approach him, and so I laid distractions aside and struck up a conversation with him. During the next twenty minutes or so we became acquainted, and I asked him if I could buy him a sandwich, which he was eager for me to do.

After handing him a breakfast sandwich, I ventured into the spiritual side of the conversation. I asked him if he had any spiritual beliefs, to which he responded positively. Then I asked him if he had placed his faith in Jesus Christ, as his Lord and Savior. His response was quick, and very amusing. He replied, "Yes, I have, I sure don't want to go through hell twice!" Given the condition he was in, I could see his point, and his response was positive and convincing . . . and very creative!

Even when the distractions of life get in the way, you can trust that God is guiding and prompting you, ready to speak whenever you are willing to listen. You are on your way to your eternal destination in heaven!

In the same way, it is your task to use the tools and equipment you have been given to accomplish God's mission of bringing others to salvation in Jesus Christ. You don't have the excuse of limited data—you have been given all the information you need in God's Word. When you share the gospel, you spread vital information that affects the eternal destination of your friends, family, coworkers, and neighbors. God has put protections in place for you when you do, that the devil will be unable to interfere with your kingdom efforts. You have the ability and equipment to bring increase and hear the words "well done," no airplane mode required.

What Will You Do to Have Your Best Life in Eternity?

1. Why do you think the rationalist businessman on the plane rejected the gospel? How would you approach an atheist whose foundation is in empirical facts rather than the Bible or the spiritual?

2. Do you fall into any of the traps from "What Gospel Sharing Is Not"? Which do you struggle with the most: sharing your testimony, the silent witness, forcing your religion on another, or inviting them to church?

3. Ponder the idea that the gospel is "good news." What does that mean to you? What does it mean for your friends, family, or neighbors?

4. What do you think it means to be an ambassador for Christ? What actions can you take? Or avoid?

5. What has been your prior experience sharing the gospel? What would you like to change anything moving forward?

6. What acts of mercy are you involved with that can create an opportunity to share Jesus?

Chapter 8
Faith Vanquishes Fear

I'm not moved by what I see, I'm not moved by what I feel, I'm moved only by the Word of God.
—Smith Wigglesworth

D. L. Moody was an impactful evangelist of the nineteenth century who virtually revolutionized evangelism in the United States. In a time with no mass media, he is said to have spoken to over one hundred thousand people. His singular text was nothing but God's Word. D. L. Moody reportedly said, "Our greatest fear should not be of failure, but of succeeding at something that doesn't really matter." Hearing Jesus tell you, "Well done," and reaping magnificent rewards for eternity *really* matter—literally for millions of years in your greater heavenly life. In chapter 7 we examined the importance of bringing increase by sharing Jesus with others. In this chapter, we will address common impediments to witnessing and how we can overcome them. While you may feel hesitant or unequipped to share your faith, the truth is that you will be surprised at the mighty ways God will use you when you do. Thankfully, God doesn't necessarily call those who are equipped; He equips those He calls. And friend, you are called to share the hope that resides in you (see 1 Peter 3:15). Sharing the gospel is not an optional feature of the Christian life. It is an essential part of living for Christ and bringing kingdom increase. Jesus was very open and forthright—kind of pointed, actually—about acknowledging Him before men: "Whoever is ashamed of Me and My words in this adulterous and sinful generation, of him the Son of Man also will be ashamed when He comes in the glory of His Father with the holy angels" (Mark 8:38).

I am looking forward to the second coming of Jesus, but this puts a different spin on it entirely. The language here references His return (see Matthew 25:31) and His displeasure with us if we are ashamed of Him before others. What does Jesus mean by *ashamed*? The original language of the Bible defines the word *ashamed* as "properly, *disgraced*, like someone 'singled out' because they *mis*placed their confidence or support ('believed the big lie'); to be ashamed (*personally* humiliated).["][1]

In other words, Jesus is saying you and I are not to be afraid to be singled out as His followers—to place our confidence in and support behind Him. We are not to be afraid of embarrassment about our association with Him. Our relationship with Jesus should be front and center; it should be clear to anyone who knows us that we are believers. The good news is that we don't need to be timid or afraid of what others may say or think of our witness. We need only to be faithful!

Eager Witnesses

The early believers were unafraid to spread the gospel, that's for sure. Under threat of imprisonment, beatings, and frequently even death, they were faithful to share the good news. Consider their shining testimonies.

In Acts 4, Peter and John, when asked to deny Jesus after having been arrested and facing the authorities, were bold in their replied: "Whether it is right in the sight of God to listen to you more than to God, you judge" (v. 19). They refused to let fear hinder their burning desire to share the good news of salvation with anyone who would listen.

In confronting the officials, the disciples often faced pressure to give in and even dealt with suffering. Acts 5:40 states, "When they had called for the apostles and beaten them, they commanded that they should not speak in the name of Jesus, and let them go." How do you think they responded? It is convicting to see that the disciples responded with joy that they were "worthy" to suffer for the gospel, and they continued preaching everywhere they went (vv. 41–42).

These guys were enthusiastic about sharing their experience of how Jesus had changed their lives! They were eager for others to know. They considered the cost and were convinced that it was of more value to share Jesus than to please the authorities of their time. Their witness of Christ was more important to them than personal reputation—even health and safety. May we have such zeal amid our darkening culture.

I for one am thankful that I am not under that kind of threat. Yet I find myself convicted that at times I have been timid in bringing up the subject of Jesus. Certainly, the cost of witnessing for Christ is very low in America, compared to what these first apostles faced. Still, this type of persecution is a reality today in our world. Being a believer—let alone a witness—in China, Iran, and Jerusalem is hazardous, even illegal. While you are reading this sentence, your brothers and sisters in Christ are imprisoned and tortured for the very same thing the believers in the era of the early church were. Yet here in America the many believers are often ashamed to even pray in public or carry a Bible—much less witness in Jesus name. Friend, I promise there is a better way; you can overcome your fear!

Jesus is serious about you sharing your faith! He is, in

essence, saying you will reap what you sow. Jesus instructed His disciples, "Whoever denies Me before men, him I will also deny before My Father who is in heaven" (Matthew 10:33). We often think of this verse in the context of not denying Him when under threat of death. But what if Jesus meant *just being afraid* of humiliation or being embarrassed to share the gospel? Certainly the price of a little embarrassment is small compared with the thought of Jesus denying you before the throne of God! So why are you timid? We should neither fear nor hesitate to share the good news!

Fear

Often underlying this reluctance is a common emotion that holds us back from bringing increase: fear. Fear is not God's design or purpose for our life. Rather, we are created by God for His kingdom's work. We have eternal blessings waiting for us and an appointed destiny to fulfill for Him. Fear is a reaction; courage is a decision. Ephesians 2:10 says, "For we are His workmanship, created in Christ Jesus for good works, which God prepared beforehand that we should walk in them."

> **Fear may be the lock on the door to our dreams. Boldness is the key.**

Even though we share common fears, we don't need to let them control our actions—not when we are in Christ! Fear may be the lock on the door to our dreams. Boldness is the key. We have been freed to share the gospel and fulfill the plans that God has for us if we have accepted Jesus finished work on the cross. You, friend, can be rewarded in heaven and hear the words "well done."

Even knowing the truth, it can be easy to allow fear to

grip you and prevent you from sharing your most treasured possession: salvation. It can be difficult to live a life set apart and faithfully witness when the world so often tells you not to. But naming your obstacles is the first step in overcoming them. So let's take a moment to examine some common fears that may be holding you back.

"I don't want to be rejected."

This is likely the most common reason you do not share your faith in Jesus Christ. It is based on the *assumption* of rejection even before you speak. But what if you chose to assume differently? What if you chose to believe that your steps are ordered by the Lord each moment of each day?[2] How would it change the way you live to assume that your encounters are God-ordained and for His eternal purposes—that the next person you bump into might already be under conviction or at least already have a seed planted in their soul, waiting for you to water? You do not know what is happening within the heart of the next person you meet. They may be under tremendous conviction, or the Holy Spirit may be drawing them with a longing they hide well. You can never know.

I'd like to share the story of twin brothers. It is a story that shows that you never know how God may use your witness:

> A young man and his twin brother lived in a large East Coast city. One of the brothers would take a bus at 5 a.m. early in the morning to work. On that bus there were typically only two people—a very attractive young lady and a very unattractive, grumpy, and hardened old man.
>
> The young man was on the shy side and really wanted to talk to the young lady and work up the courage

to build a relationship. He also felt a conviction to share Jesus Christ with the old man on the bus. Months and months went by—even a year—without his sharing a word with either. As time went on, he got a promotion and a job in another city. Then the day came he knew would be his last ride on the bus. He never worked up the courage to talk to the girl, but before his last stop, he worked up the courage to go up to the old man, sit down beside him, and share his faith in Jesus Christ. In a surprising display of anger and rejection, the old man soundly and profanely reviled him. The young man then quickly exited the bus.

Years went by. One day his twin brother was giving a testimony at a local church in that city. At the end of the service an aged man came up to his twin brother. He said, "Do you remember me?" The brother said no. He said, "Let me refresh your memory. I am the old man who was on the bus several years ago that you came up to and shared Jesus Christ with. I wanted to apologize to you, for I mistreated you horribly that day. But what you didn't know is that I was already under a tremendous burden of conviction by God to turn my life over to Christ, and that night before I went to bed, I wrestled with the Holy Spirit and surrendered my life to Jesus Christ! Thank you for being bold enough and caring enough to share with me!" The twin brother quickly realized that, though it wasn't him, it was most likely his brother who had moved to a different city.

We should assume the best will happen and lead with the faith that it is always right to winsomely share, even when the situation seems hopeless. Scripture encourages us to be quick with an answer and eager to share Jesus Christ: "Preach the word! Be ready in season and out of season. Convince, rebuke, exhort, with all longsuffering and teaching" (2 Timothy 4:2). Through Jesus teachings, it is evident that sharing the gospel is a vital component of the Christian life.

> Sharing has benefits for both parties involved.

I've had the honor of sharing Jesus with hundreds of people. Thankfully (and I have found most commonly), I have *never* experienced a hostile response. But I am willing to face embarrassment or rejection for the sake of another's salvation. The end result is better for both of us! This is the way that we are able to bring kingdom increase—when we place the gospel in the center of our life. We are blessed when we do!

"I don't want to be embarrassed."

Another common fear is being asked a question you may be unable to answer. You fear not being familiar enough with the Word of God to wisely respond to hard questions. A good thing to remember about witnessing is that you are not obligated to be a theologian or an expert on the Bible and that being stumped with a question is unlikely. Think about it. Most people you meet have likely not been in church for years—if ever! You have been going weekly (or at least regularly). You have a real knowledge advantage—and they likely would not even know if you did give an incomplete answer or couldn't quote God's Word precisely! While this advantage is not an excuse to avoid wrestling with difficult questions, it is a reassurance that you don't need to have all of the answers to be an effective witness for Christ and earn heavenly rewards.

On rare occasions, people will ask me difficult questions,

such as "Why does God let children be killed by Hamas?" I count this as spiritual warfare of sorts. When you focus the conversation on Jesus, sometimes you will be thrown a question that pulls the conversation away from Him. I believe it is because the other person is feeling the conviction of the Holy Spirit, and the Enemy knows that questions can distract or even derail the person's chance to hear the gospel. Be persistent to lovingly lead them back to the subject at hand—Jesus Christ—and focus on how they are going to respond to His redemptive work on the cross.

"I don't want to get into an argument."
The gospel is not about pushing another into your worldview. When someone takes the time to communicate important truth, it may be misjudged. Others might mistake your concern and outreach as fanaticism. Still, it is true you sincerely want to give others the best thing in your life: Jesus.

Because this breaks so clearly with our culture, you need to know that it is both acceptable and not fanatical. You are *not* shoving religion down anyone's throat when you talk about your faith. In fact, you do not have a religion at all. Loving Jesus is a *relationship*, not merely a religion or collection of beliefs—it is more like a marriage.

The world may attempt to brand you as a fanatic for sharing your faith in Christ. But when you know the pitfalls to avoid, you can talk about your relationship with Jesus confidently, without worrying that you will be categorized in this way. I recently found this account in a posting from *Relevant* magazine of what a fanatic might look like:

> I was walking down the sidewalk where these two men still stood, still waving their signs and still motioning

at cars as they drove by. As I approached, one of them yelled toward me, "Pray for revival brother!" I sheepishly smiled, avoided eye contact, and picked up the pace in my walk. As I passed by him, he turned toward me and yelled again, "Pray for revival BROTHER!" Scared me to death.

A few days later, Chris, one of the guys on staff, attended a Braves baseball game. During the seventh inning stretch the same guy appeared, but this time running across the field frantically waving a "JESUS LOVES YOU" sign.

Security chased him down, tackled him, and dragged him kicking and fighting off the field.

As Chris told me the story, I shook my head in disbelief. What could go through someone's mind to make them think doing something like that is in any way positive? Is it really making a difference in eternity? All I can see it doing is giving you a jail record.[3]

While most believers could be categorized as the polar opposite in never sharing their faith, this guy is an over-the-top example of a fanatical approach. Sharing with others about your relationship with your best friend, Jesus, is important to God and benefits the lost around you. But "arguing them down," twisting their arm, or forcing your opinion is the wrong approach. I love the saying "A man persuaded against his will is of the same opinion still."[4] Your purpose is to speak of the hope that you have and let God change the other person's heart. Scripture calls you to view others as your neighbors and treat them with respect, as Jesus did. Jesus was loving but truthful. So should your witness also be.

What you have to offer is life and joy—for this world and

the one beyond. I've never had to argue when giving someone a freshly baked chocolate chip cookie, and this is far better. You are sharing good news that others need to hear. Still, the Holy Spirit is a gentleman in the sense that He will never go where He is unwelcome or shoulder His way into someone's life. If the person you are talking to has earnest questions, you absolutely can respond. But to push your faith on another is unnecessary. Why?

Because the issue here is more than mental assent to the argument of Jesus deity and saviorhood. A heart change must occur. Heart change is different from intellectual knowledge. A person may mentally accept the gospel but not trust God, surrender their will, or love Jesus. This is the work only the Holy Spirit can accomplish.

Friend, your job is to sow seeds. You must speak the truth in love and allow, as well as be sensitive to, the Holy Spirit to bring conviction. Some say the biggest distance in humanity is the twelve inches between the mind and the heart. If you will consider and act on the simple strategy found in the following chapters, you will see God use you to bridge that gap, convicting and changing many hearts. You will find that God will do the work of persuasion; your job is to set forth loving truth. In so doing you will bring increase that will be rewarded on that great day before the heavenly throne!

Once you have set the truth and an opportunity to accept Jesus gift of salvation before another in a winsome and loving fashion, your part is done. We see this in the Bible often. For instance, take Paul's encounter with Agrippa.[5] He shared the gospel, Agrippa was convicted, yet he was lost. Paul didn't push; he just spoke the truth. In the same way, you only need to be faithful to speak about Jesus.

The point is that fear of argumentation is based on the beliefs that others are contentious and that it is your responsibility to get them saved. Neither one is true! I truly have never encountered a person responding with anger. And while you are asked to "contend earnestly for the faith which was once for all delivered to the saints" (Jude 3), you do so while working alongside the conviction and power of the Holy Spirit. Only through the work of the Holy Spirit are you able to bring kingdom increase and keep the gospel in its proper place in your life to bring blessing.

"Well Done, Good and Faithful Servant"

Did you know that God intentionally places lost people in your life? By entering into conversations with them, you are obeying the Great Commission—which is Jesus last commandment—and bringing eternal increase. Witnessing puts you in the center of God's greatest purpose: to save humanity. Too often the fears listed in the preceding pages hold you back from eternal blessing and an abundant life of fruitfulness in Jesus. God wants more for your life than to be bound by fear. As we return to the parable of the talents, notice the words that Jesus used on this topic.

Consider the words of the third servant in the previously mentioned parable: "I was *afraid*, and went and hid your talent in the ground" (Matthew 25:25, emphasis mine). This guy's primary motivation for hiding his master's money was fear. You need to be careful that you do not hide the best thing God has entrusted to you—salvation. It is meant to be shared and to multiply! In contrast to his words to the servants who brought increase, the master's words to the third servant were harsh: "You wicked and lazy servant" (v. 26). Those certainly aren't the words you want to hear when you arrive in heaven! The worker, moved by fear, didn't want to extend the effort to risk multiplying the treasure he had. Let's not make the same mistake with the treasure God has given us.

In His Word, God deals very directly with the subject of fear. In fact, "do not be afraid" is one of the most frequent commands in the Bible.[6] The phrase "fear not" is found in sixty-three verses (in the King James Version). I think God is trying to warn us that fear robs us of the ability to delight His heart. Remember the words spoken to the servants who brought increase: "Enter into the joy of your lord" (Matthew 25:21, 23). What a great thought—to bring joy to God! We need to abandon fear and boldly share Jesus! If you are to hear the words "well done, good and faithful servant" and receive eternal blessings, you must bring increase with your life. To bring increase, you must allow God to do His good work in you to transform your heart. Notice that each of the fears listed above is self-centered:

- I don't want to be rejected.
- I don't want to be embarrassed.
- I don't want to get into an argument.

Self-focus is contrary to Jesus' teachings. Instead, "Jesus said to His disciples, 'If anyone desires to come after Me, let him deny himself, and take up his cross, and follow Me. For whoever desires to save his life will lose it, but whoever loses his life for My sake will find it'" (Matthew 16:24–25).

Being a faithful witness will require you to put your*self* on the line for Jesus, like He did for you. There is nothing more important to God than the lordship of Christ in your life. This is clear in Ephesians 1:10, which says, "In the dispensation of the fullness of the times He might gather together in one all things in Christ, both which are in heaven and which are on earth—in Him." The increase that pleases God and brings joy is the increase of Christ's lordship in others He died for. We have seen that fear is a pervading hindrance in bringing increase—

and an issue God frequently commanded against in His Word. Whether it is fear of rejection, embarrassment, or getting into an argument, these fears are all based on self-protection.

Fear may be the primary reason you are reluctant to share about Jesus, or there may be another cause. Here are a few other stumbling blocks, which I refer to as cultural Christian nonstarters, that hinder or attempt to excuse witnessing for Jesus. As you read, consider fear's place in your heart and whether one of these other obstacles is holding you back from sharing the gospel and receiving "an eternal reward".

"I'm not a good enough Christian."
Biblical faith comes through the Word of God; it cannot be conveyed and is not validated by our actions alone. While you can (and should) display Christ's virtues, an understanding and conviction of His atoning life, death, and resurrection must be communicated through words. Look again at the enthusiasm of the apostles regarding verbally sharing Jesus message: "We cannot but speak the things which we have seen and heard" (Acts 4:20). Jesus Himself insisted on the hearing of His words for eternal life: "Most assuredly, I say to you, he who hears My word and believes in Him who sent Me has everlasting life, and shall not come into judgment, but has passed from death into life" (John 5:24).

Friend, this is a relief. You and I do not have to (and frankly cannot) live a sinless life. If my acquaintance's eternal destiny is dependent on my conduct, we all will be disappointed! God did not leave such important matters to the hazards of sinful humans. He gave us His Word and the Holy Spirit to bring about conviction and salvation. Speaking of our Helper (the Holy Spirit) in these matters, Jesus said, "Nevertheless I tell you the truth. It is to your advantage that I go away; for if I do not go away, the Helper will not come to you; but if I depart, I will send Him to you. And when He has come, He will convict the world of sin, and of righteousness, and of judgment" (John 16:7–8).

Thankfully the burden to convict another of their need for Christ is not dependent on a well-lived life or on our powers of persuasion. It is dependent on the Word of God and the Holy Spirit. Salvation is from the Lord. While we have a responsibility to share, ultimately no one comes to the Lord unless He draws them, and the vehicle is God's Word, not our actions alone. John 6:44 tells us, "No one can come to Me unless the Father who sent Me draws him; and I will raise him up at the last day."

If God is the One responsible to save people, your part is easy—just speak the truth! You are not obligated to model, persuade, or convict others. You don't have to be a "good enough" Christian. You are only offering the best thing anyone has ever offered a lost friend or acquaintance: eternal life. You simply put it out there and let the Spirit and the Word of God do the heavy lifting.

To remove Scripture from the salvation process removes the very power of the process: "For the word of God is living and powerful, and sharper than any two-edged sword, piercing even to the division of soul and spirit, and of joints and marrow, and is a discerner of the thoughts and intents of the heart" (Hebrews 4:12). Your responsibility is to sow the Word of God before others. He is the One who does the work to change hearts. This means that being "good enough" is not necessary! This is good news: every believer is qualified to share the gospel.

"Everyone is saved and a child of God."

It may seem "the gift of the obvious" to you, but this belief is found among many who claim faith in Christ. Perhaps it stems from the thought that God is, in the sense of being Creator, the Father of all, because He indeed made us all. It is true that God is the Creator and knit you together in your mother's womb (see Psalm 139). You have been wonderfully made by God. Yet Scripture clearly contradicts the idea that everyone inherits eternal life. The fact that God made each of us does not diminish the sinful state of humanity:

> In which you once walked according to the course of this world, according to the prince of the power of the air, the spirit who now works in the sons of disobedience, among whom also we all once conducted ourselves in the lusts of our flesh, fulfilling the desires of the flesh and of the mind, and were by nature children of wrath, just as the others. (Ephesians 2:2–3)

Jesus Himself made it clear that there needs to be a transformation in your life. As we saw in chapter 5, you and I must be spiritually reborn to enter the kingdom of God. Without the new birth, everyone on the planet is unsaved.

> Jesus answered and said to him, "Most assuredly, I say to you, unless one is born again, he cannot see the kingdom of God."
> Nicodemus said to Him, "How can a man be born when he is old? Can he enter a second time into his mother's womb and be born?"
> Jesus answered, "Most assuredly, I say to you, unless one is born of water and the Spirit, he cannot enter the kingdom of God." (John 3:3–5)

We mentioned earlier that there are only two kinds of people on earth today: those who are born again and those who need to be. Here is the reality of the two kinds of people you will meet:

1. Those who have experienced the new birth and are going to heaven. The Word makes it clear: "As many as received Him, to them He gave the right to become children of God, to those who believe in His name" (John 1:12). If they are fellow believers, you can fellowship and edify each other.

2. Those who are only "born of water"; they have not experienced the new birth and are destined for eternal alienation from the God who created them. In the words of Jesus, "You must be born again." This is why Christ came: to offer us admittance into a new kingdom that is not of this world. Remember His words to Pilate during His trial: "My kingdom is not of this world. If My kingdom were of this world, My servants would fight, so that I should not be delivered to the Jews; but now My kingdom is not from here" (John 18:36).

The reality that not everyone is in Jesus kingdom and has been saved should set us ablaze with urgency. We've seen that we are ambassadors of God's heavenly kingdom and that each person on earth must be born again in order to access it. You and I hold the key to their entrance; it is the gospel.

"I'll share next time."

John Wooden said, "Do not let what you cannot do interfere with what you can do." The instances where I have disregarded this sound advice probably number in the dozens. Thinking I'll share next time may look like this: I get into a conversation with a coworker (or whomever), and small talk runs its course. Then I feel it: the conviction (which I believe is from the Holy Spirit) to share my love for and faith in Jesus Christ. I know this person is not saved. I am concerned and have prayed for them. I am with them relatively alone now . . . but I let the moment pass without sharing. Generally, my reasoning is that "I will do it at a better or another time. I will have another chance." Of all the nonstarters to sharing your faith, this is likely one of the most common.

This is a common excuse because it relieves the pressure of taking that step to share. While I do not believe you will be effective if you are sharing under compulsion or pressure, the reality is, tomorrow is not a sure thing. You may never see this person again. They may move, quit, even die . . . and you will have missed the chance. Your urgency to seize the moment is born out of a heart of compassion for those God has sovereignly put in your path—not out of compulsion alone. You share because the love of Christ compels you (see 2 Corinthians 5:14). The opportunity to share your love for Jesus, especially when you feel that small tug of the Spirit, may never come again. God is sovereign; He controls *all things*—even your opportunities for conversation. He works all things "according to the counsel of His will" (Ephesians 1:11).

I encourage and challenge you to look at life as a God-ordained adventure. Tomorrow, consider everyone you meet as being sent by God, every conversation you have as a divine appointment. Ask yourself: What is God's purpose for my meeting this person? How can I work together with Him to accomplish His purpose? When you do, you will be placing the gospel in its proper place in your life and will be rewarded in heaven for the increase that you bring.

In this chapter, we have identified some common beliefs which can cause you not to speak about God's Word and the gospel. I believe most of us as Christ-followers would delight in seeing friends and relatives come to know Jesus. God put you in their lives so they can know Him! Though I believe there are few who would deliberately use the nonstarters mentioned as an open excuse to disobey Jesus' command, the reasoning causes you to be a little too comfortable in avoiding conversations about the gospel. It is our imperative as Christians to spread this good news! In the following chapter, we will share easy, biblical tools for witnessing.

Departures

TIME	TO	GATE	REMARK
10:00	HEAVEN	A10	DELAYED
10:02	HEAVEN	A03	ON-TIME
10:08	HEAVEN	A06	CANCELED
10:09	HEAVEN	A12	ON-TIME
10:12	HEAVEN	B07	ON-TIME
10:14	HEAVEN	B02	DELAYED
10:21	HEAVEN	H07	ON-TIME

Experiencing Turbulence

Hearing the flight attendant announce that we will be hitting a patch of turbulence can be frightening. Turbulence shakes up the status quo and is a reminder that you have not yet safely reached your destination. Similarly, God can use difficult circumstances to shake you out of your comfort zone and remind you that this earthly life is not lasting. The work of the Holy Spirit shifts your perspective and brings uncomfortable moments of conviction. But it is always for your good!

I distinctly remember the time I was in a small Tennessee tourist town called Pigeon Forge. I was there with my family on vacation, and there were the typical time-share booths with bright pictures of tropical beaches adorning most of the gift shop areas. As my wife and daughters walked into one of those crowded gift shops, I noticed that there was a time-share guy looking directly at me from behind the colorful booth in front of the store. I determined that I would walk around that booth, as I was not interested in the presentation and the free whatever offering that day.

However, I felt the nudge of the Holy Spirit. I hesitated, and I'll admit that some nonstarters ran through my mind. I honestly didn't want to go up to him in that moment. I wanted to enjoy my time doing activities with my family, rather than go up to a stranger who was trying to sell me something. But again, even more strongly, I felt the conviction on my heart to go speak with him. And so I did. I listened dutifully to his time-share presentation, despite being uninterested in the product, because I knew that God had a purpose in drawing me to interact with this man. As he was speaking, the Holy Spirit brought up this thought in my mind: *This man has had a difficult life.*

After he was done with his presentation, I asked him a question: "Jason, it seems to me that you've had a difficult road to travel in your life, is that right?"

He looked at me strangely and then said what so many often do on being confronted with a supernaturally revealed fact: "How did you know that?" I explained that it was a thought from the Holy Spirit.

He went on to tell me, "Yeah, I've been in prison. In fact, I just got out about a year ago, but you know, it wasn't that bad in prison, actually. I'm part of a Bible study, and things were really better than they are now. I've kind of fallen back into some of the same patterns that I had before I went in."

Like He did in that situation, God knows when you are struggling to share, and He knows who is struggling in their faith. Miraculously, He will lead you into opportunities to bless you both! When you feel the conviction of the Holy Spirit, know that you are about to be transformed more into the likeness of Christ. This will bring you eternal blessing and potentially eternity for another!

What Will You Do to Have Your Best Life in Eternity?

1. Would you describe yourself as an eager witness for the gospel? Why or why not? How do you tend to react when in conversation with a nonbeliever?

2. Which of the nonstarters hinders you the most? Fear of rejection, embarrassment, getting into an argument, not feeling good enough, believing everyone is already saved, putting actions over words, or waiting to share next time?

3. Which would you rather face—the risk of your sharing being rejected by another or the risk of displeasing Jesus when you stand before Him?

4. Do you have faith that God is able to give you the right words to say when telling another of your love for Christ, or do you feel like it is dependent on you alone?

5. Are you willing to risk embarrassment, inconvenience, or, at worst, antagonism from another for the sake of their salvation? For the sake of the gospel?

6. How does the joy of knowing you're saved make sharing easier to do? Does knowing we are simply "seed sowers" relieve any pressure in sharing the gospel?

Chapter 9
Eternity's Invitation

He who wins souls is wise.

—*Proverbs 11:30*

God doesn't evaluate wisdom the way we do. He doesn't look for a PhD, earthly success, a perfect image, or outward strength. God created you in the context of His divine wisdom, a wisdom with eternity in mind. He knew you before the foundation of the world. He knew why the world needed you—yes, *you*—at this time, in this place, for His purposes and glory. Only you can live in the way He has destined for you; no one else can. That's the highest purpose He created you for.

David the shepherd-king is a great example of living in divine wisdom to fulfill God's purpose. Acts 13 describes him in this way: "David, after he had served his own generation by the will of God, fell asleep, was buried with his fathers" (v. 36). It is recorded in Scripture for posterity that God created David for a specific purpose in his time and place and that David *fulfilled* the purpose God had destined for him. David was just a shepherd boy minding the lambs when the unexpected destiny of God came upon his life. Arguably he was the runt of the family. His brothers were older, taller, and the more logical choice to become rulers. But God saw differently than man; He knew David was a man after His own heart. He chose David and destined him to be a prophet, warrior, priest, and the greatest king ever seated on the throne of Israel. This was all preset for him while he was still a little shepherd boy alone in the field.[1]

It's the same for you—David is no different than you are! You may look at the circumstances of your life and feel a long way from greatness or any divine plan. But don't believe it. God has specifically gifted you with His Holy Spirit, His Word, the people you meet, and the circumstances He's allowed in your life to fulfill His destiny. That destiny is found singularly in His purposes. As we have seen, the greatest purpose God has for you is to glorify His Son through your testimony. As you live to honor and bring attention to Jesus, He will honor you. In fact, that is His promise in Scripture: "But now the Lord says: 'Far be it from Me; for those who honor Me I will honor'" (1 Samuel 2:30). To be honored by God is a blessing beyond all comparison, holding value not only for life here on earth, but especially for rewards in heaven. But admittedly, being a bold witness for Christ can be challenging.

In the last chapter we looked at a number of common misconceptions and apprehensions that can impede our progress of sharing the gospel. Importantly, we've also seen in previous chapters that being a faithful steward of the gospel has an enormous impact on rewards, the quality of our life for eternity, and hearing the words "well done." Still, it can be intimidating to talk about salvation with others. But there's good news: God is preparing your heart and giving you the tools to share His message with those around you. God is setting you up for the purpose of witnessing. He has equipped you with the Holy Spirit to witness . . . it is scriptural:

God has revealed them to us through His Spirit. For the Spirit searches all things, yes, the deep things of God. For what man knows the things of a man except the spirit of the man which is in him? Even so no one knows the things of God except the Spirit of God. Now we have received, not the spirit of the world, but the Spirit who is from God, that we might know the things that have been freely given to us by God. (1 Corinthians 2:10–12)

God knows your heart, understands your apprehensions and desires. He also knows what is best for each person you meet. His Holy Spirit, working through the Word and external circumstances, can powerfully convict those you interact with, using you to intimately touch their hearts. You simply must be open to it. In being open to sharing the good news, you can have two of the most exciting experiences in life: (1) seeing God at work in another, because conversion is God-dependent, not man-dependent, and (2) God using you to deeply touch a person's heart.

Two Ways to Witness

Because sharing our faith is so important and yet at times awkward, I want to explore two simple ways we can witness: a Scripture-centered way and a Holy Spirit–centered way.

1. Let the Bible, God's Word, do the work.

This is a simple way to break into a spiritual conversation with another, because often just switching into spiritual subject matter can be an awkward thing to do. First, obtain a few Gideon New Testaments. These New Testaments are an easy-to-use witnessing tool, putting God's Word into the other person's hand even after you're done with your interaction. Many Gideon New Testaments have two components, in addition to a full copy of the New Testament. The first component, in the front of the book, is an index. This index has a diverse list of subjects and what the Bible says about them, including the page and Scripture reference. The Gideon New Testament also has a Romans Road feature in the back.[2] The Romans Road exposits the atoning work of Christ and the need for repentance from sin. Let me demonstrate with a personal story about how you can use this book to witness.

I was recently in a restaurant with the men's group from our ministry. We had an effusive, gregarious waiter who was a lot of fun. After dinner all the men left, but I felt a burden to go talk with the waiter, thank him for serving our table, and ask how he was doing. After we had chatted for a bit, he mentioned some discord in his family. I said, "I have a gift for you," and handed him a Gideon New Testament. I asked, "Do you have one of these?" He said he didn't. I replied, "Well, that's my gift to you. Do you know what it is?" He said, "It looks like a Bible." I told him, "Yes, this is a book inspired by God Himself, every word. I want to show you something neat about this book. Here in the front is an index that has answers to many of life's issues, such as addictions, anger, divorce. The index tells you where to find what God has to say about them and how He can help you." The waiter liked that concept, particularly given his family struggles. At this point he was happy to receive the book.

Then I said, "If you think that's great, there's something even better." I turned to the back of the book and told him, "Here in this section are instructions on how you can *live forever*. You know, we're all going to die someday." He acknowledged that reality. I continued, "Everyone has always wanted to know how to live forever, and this is the path to eternal life." I shared the Romans Road and asked if he wanted to put his faith in Jesus Christ.

Offering a Bible as a gift is a low-stress way to engage people. I've never had anyone turn down a gift! It is a great icebreaker for a spiritual conversation and is an effective witnessing tool, because you have placed the living Word in their hands. God can even work through that Bible in their future, beyond your meeting. All this method takes is a bit of your desire to share and some holy boldness to engage in conversation and offer this gift. The Romans Road explains itself, and after you've shared it, just ask if they want to place their trust and faith for salvation in Jesus Christ. If they answer yes, pray together. God may use you with this tool to witness the conversion of a soul!

2. Let the Holy Spirit do the work.

As I've mentioned before, *conversion depends on God.* He is the only One who can bring about salvation. Scripture tells us, "No one can come to Me unless the Father who sent Me draws him" (John 6:44). God seeks the lost; He is the shepherd. You join in His process as you depend on Him. Recall what I did before I spoke with the businessman on the plane: I prayed. I asked for God's wisdom. Notice what God did: He brought a relevant thought which the man was already contemplating to mind, revealing truth. When I listened and spoke aloud what God prompted, it touched the man deeply. This would not have been possible without the supernatural work of the living God.

The Holy Spirit's Purpose

In Christian culture, the Holy Spirit has been represented as a healer, a heavenly tongues–giver, a prophecy-giver, and other manifestations, which some embrace while others reject. But Scripture reveals a higher purpose for the Holy Spirit in your life.

Biblically, what is the Holy Spirit's purpose for being with you on earth? We can easily find the answer to this in the Word of God. Jesus told us directly. It is to disclose God's will to you.

He can speak. When the Holy Spirit reveals something, He has a purpose: to glorify Christ. Jesus said this: "He will glorify Me, for He will take of what is Mine and declare it to you. All things that the Father has are Mine. Therefore I said that He will take of Mine and declare it to you" (John 16:14–15). So the Spirit of God exists to disclose Jesus. Here is life's greatest adventure and privilege: to let the Holy Spirit reveal truth about another person that will glorify Jesus!

The principle is that God does the drawing through the Holy Spirit, apart from human devices. This is what the apostle Paul meant when he said we are laborers together with God (see 1 Corinthians 3:9). This is also what he meant when he said that we are ministers of reconciliation, as if God were appealing *through us* on Christ's behalf to be reconciled to God (see 2 Corinthians 5). In all these things, we see that the Holy Spirit drawing others to salvation in Christ is from the Lord and not from us.

> **The Spirit of God exists to disclose Jesus.**

God Is Alive

It's easy to go about your life without grasping the reality that the almighty God of the universe is alive and intimately involved in every detail. But it's true. God is overwhelmingly thinking about you every moment. We find this verified in Psalm 139, which says that God's thoughts about you number more than the grains of sand at the sea! He is indeed living and active. I recently learned another name of our God: El Chay. This term means God the Living, or the Living God.[3] First Samuel 17:26 says, "Then David spoke to the men who stood by him, saying, 'What shall be done for the man who kills this Philistine and takes away the reproach from Israel? For who is this uncircumcised Philistine, that he should defy the armies of [El Chay]?'"

If God is alive (which is true!), then He is involved in all circumstances regarding our lives and eternity. By being sensitive to the Holy Spirit's work and speaking biblical truth, you can reach people right where they are. This assures that God alone gets the glory for revealing something that will touch their heart. Here is a simple, God-dependent way that allows the Holy Spirit to use you in sharing Jesus with others: (1) pray, (2) listen, (3) speak, and (4) invite. Let's look at the first three steps in more depth and then (4) invite in the next chapter.

1. Pray

Rather than depend on your memory of God's Word or the Romans Road[4] or another method, you can pray. Ask God to reveal a verse or give insight into something the person may have said, or an observation that might be a gateway to their heart. Ask God to bring to your awareness anything He would have you know. God knows it all: "And there is no creature hidden from His sight, but all things are naked and open to the eyes of Him to whom we must give account" (Hebrews 4:13).

As you seek discernment and wait for God to show you an opening to someone's heart, pray that God will open their eyes. Scripture tells us the unbelieving are blinded to the truth—the lost cannot see the light of the gospel. But the gospel has power to open blind eyes. God is able and willing to help unbelievers see the truth of the gospel as you call on His name "to open their eyes, in order to turn them from darkness to light, and from the power of Satan to God, that they may receive forgiveness of sins and an inheritance among those who are sanctified by faith in Me" (Acts 26:18). They are unable to believe on their own because the things of God are foolishness to them (see 1 Corinthians 2:14).

Scripture also describes this using the image of a veil: "But even if our gospel is veiled, it is veiled to those who are perishing, whose minds the god of this age has blinded, who do not believe, lest the light of the gospel of the glory of Christ, who is the image of God, should shine on them" (2 Corinthians 4:3–4). You can pray that God lifts this veil and reveals truth, opening their eyes to spiritual reality, bringing them out of darkness, and delivering them from Satan's grip and into the kingdom of God, that they might receive forgiveness. That is the power of prayer. You, friend, have the Holy Spirit working through you! The exciting thing is that this is the work of God—only He can open blind eyes, lift the veil, and draw unbelievers to Himself. Every true soul-winner understands that salvation comes only from God. "No one can come to Me unless the Father who sent Me draws him; and I will raise him up at the last day" (John 6:44).

> **Every true soul-winner understands that salvation comes only from God.**

Praying when you encounter another person formally invites God's involvement into the situation. It expresses your dependence on Him and honors Him. The Holy Spirit knows everything going on with the person you meet. He is able to reveal things to you as you interact with others:

> "Eye has not seen, nor ear heard, nor have entered into the heart of man the things which God has prepared for those who love Him." But God has revealed them to us through His Spirit. For the Spirit searches all things, yes, the deep things of God. (1 Corinthians 2:9–10)

God knows the intimate details of your life: your heart, your joy, your longings. And He knows this for everyone else as well. He is able to reveal those things to us as we seek to share with others. First Corinthians 2:11–12 tells us, "For what man knows the things of a man except the spirit of the man which is in him? Even so no one knows the things of God except the Spirit of God. Now we have received . . . the Spirit who is from God, that we might know the things that have been freely given to us by God."

Your prayer does not have to be some "hit your knees" dramatic prayer. Rather it may be a quick, in-the-moment thought-prayer, shot up to heaven, saying, "God, help me to know if there's anything about this person You'd like to reveal to me or any Scripture You'd have me share." Remember, you are praying to the living God who wants to use you to increase His kingdom!

2. Listen

After praying, listen. This "pray, then listen" process can open one of the most exciting adventures of your life—partnering with God Almighty in His changing a heart. You can participate in seeing hearts healed and restored, even an individual's eternal destination changed, as you listen to the Holy Spirit. It is God's design and desire to work with you: "I planted, Apollos watered, but God gave the increase. . . . We are God's fellow workers" (1 Corinthians 3:6, 9). Now, some might say, "I am not sure I can hear God's voice." I am not suggesting that you will hear an audible voice, but God most certainly is capable of prompting a thought or helping you see the relevance of a comment someone has made, which will open a special door to witness.

God's chosen instruments to change hearts are Christians like us! You can be part of His work if you involve Him in your daily encounters and *listen* to His voice. What are you listening for? Well, the first and most important thing to listen for is something from God's Word. God has likely poured years of sermons, Bible study, and Christian programming into your life. The Holy Spirit can softly bring a verse or biblical story from your memory that will fit the moment and convict the one you are witnessing to: "A word fitly spoken is like apples of gold in settings of silver" (Proverbs 25:11).

God's chosen and best promptings come from the Bible, His Word. The Word has innate power to dramatically change hearts. Hebrews 4:12 reminds us that "the word of God is living and powerful, and sharper than any two-edged sword, piercing even to the division of soul and spirit, and of joints and marrow, and is a discerner of the thoughts and intents of the heart."

Scripture can instantly bring conviction and change the whole dynamic of a conversation. Bringing God's Word into the conversation is always a good idea. For example, you can say, "I have a thought I would love to share with you if you are interested." Or you can ask, "May I share with you a truth I have found about what we are discussing?" Then be a faithful witness to share it.

I remember a time when I was in the back of an Uber car heading to the Black Forest of Colorado late at night. I was about ready to snooze in the back seat when I felt a burden in my heart to talk to the driver. As we were speaking, I silently prayed, and the thought came to my mind that he was raised in a Christian home. Though he had said nothing about his homelife, I was burdened to ask. Acting on this prompting, which I felt was from the Lord, I asked, "So you were raised in a Christian home, right?"

A bit surprised, he said, "Yes, as a matter of fact, my dad is still a Baptist preacher!"

Through the rest of the drive I found out that he was not walking with the Lord as he did when he was younger, but he had been convicted of his sin over the past few months. The trip culminated in a prayer and challenge to rededicate his life to Christ. Because I listened to the Holy Spirit, the Uber driver had a supernatural encounter that evening. Only God could have revealed this knowledge—and so the man's heart was trusting and receptive. I then had a platform to share God's love and invite him to rededicate his life to the gospel of Jesus Christ. He listened, and I prayed with the driver. How exciting for both of us! You, too, can experience the Holy Spirit's involvement in conversations with others. After you pray while meeting someone, *listen.* I assure you that if your heart is inclined, God certainly is willing to speak directly to and through you. Jesus promised this: "The Holy Spirit will teach you in that very hour what you ought to say" (Luke 12:12). Friend, you only need to listen to hear from Him.

> **God can speak to you!**

It is important that I take a moment to address the common theological belief that God gave His full revelation in the Bible and that it *completed* His communication with humankind. I believe that God's authoritative revelation to humanity is found in the Bible alone, which is the only inspired and inerrant Word of God. Period. It is the *logos*, the revelation of God, and the yardstick by which we determine the validity of all that is thought to be God's will.

But God didn't send Jesus to complete His revelation and then leave us *alone.* To the contrary, He told us, "I will not leave you orphans; I will come to you" (John 14:18). Jesus indeed said He was leaving . . . and He did. He is at this moment seated at the right hand of the Father, interceding for you. But He made wonderful provision in His absence. John 14:16 says, "I will pray the Father, and He will give you another Helper, that He may abide with you forever." Jesus sent the Holy Spirit to come alongside and comfort you. The Holy Spirit came to all believers throughout time and is here as you read this book.

Jesus said it was better that He leave and send the Spirit:

"Nevertheless I tell you the truth. It is to your advantage that I go away; for if I do not go away, the Helper will not come to you; but if I depart, I will send Him to you" (John 16:7). Why is it better? Because the Spirit will "guide you into all truth; for He will not speak on His own authority, but whatever He hears He will speak; and He will tell you things to come" (John 16:13). God is alive and active in your life through the Spirit, who leads you through godly teaching, counsel, and authority, to name a few. In fact, in all of heaven and earth, He can use and receive all things to accomplish His will: "We have obtained an inheritance, being predestined according to the purpose of Him who works all things according to the counsel of His will" (Ephesians 1:11).

These verses give God's assurance that the Holy Spirit will guide you in this process of witnessing. The Holy Spirit is God's active agent on earth who reveals truth. Truth is not found exclusively in the Bible. For instance, there are facts about the world around you that you can verify, such as the shape of the sun, mathematical equations, or the idea that light is composed of photons. In the same way, statements like "you were raised in a Christian home" or "she is struggling with her health" can be true. Facts can stand without contradiction to and completely independent of the Bible. The Holy Spirit is willing to reveal facts to you—He knows everything about everyone! But you have to be listening. So, as you meet others, offer up a quick thought-prayer, asking for God's help. Listen to what the Holy Spirit may bring to your attention—maybe something they may be saying, or any verse or thought that comes to mind. Remember to test what you sense God might be prompting, making sure it aligns with Scripture. Then be faithful to witness. God will help you.

My conversation with the Uber driver who rededicated his life to Jesus demonstrates how the Holy Spirit helps us in witnessing. Notice the power of what happened during this encounter. God revealed a fact about his past that I couldn't have known. I was not aware of his background, but the Spirit revealed truth to me when I asked. That is a relief and good news! God wants you to be a successful witness for Jesus. You don't have to know Scripture perfectly or be ready with a strategy to lead people to Christ or depend on some human formula. While having a strategy or using a gospel method is fine, God is present in the moment, and He is not dependent on a method you've memorized. He is able to divinely align a verse or something the person says at that very moment.

The strategy of simply praying and listening provides the framework for a deliberate and intentional reliance on God to access truth you otherwise may be unaware of. Praying and listening is an invitation to allow His involvement in the process of witnessing. After all, He is the living God, and salvation is His idea. God literally *created* the person you are witnessing to and knows every intimate detail about them. He was there from before they were born and will be with them on the day they leave the earth. How exciting, then, to think that God can partner with you and give you knowledge that otherwise would not be part of the conversation. He can reveal the secrets and hurts of the other person's heart. This changes the conversation dramatically when the person you are witnessing to encounters God's involvement in the interaction.

3. *Speak*

God's involvement can provide you with confidence for the next step in witnessing: *speak*! After praying and listening for any insight the Holy Spirit might reveal, you should share what you believe God is giving you in the encounter. This can often be the hardest part of the process, as we saw with the nonstarters from chapter 8. So often our fears deny us, as well as the person we are with, a miraculous experience with God. To speak with confidence takes the faith that God is at work in your conversation. You must have confidence that the thought or verse that comes to mind is from the Lord. If what you think you hear is not from the Lord, nothing is lost; you simply tried but were in error. But if it is indeed from God, that can be life-changing.

God wants to meet others in an intimate and personal way. You can be the channel for His encounter with that lost coworker or friend . . . if you are willing to risk speaking Scripture or truth revealed by the Holy Spirit.

Recently, I was riding in an Uber car in Los Angeles. I was tired, jet-lagged, and not really interested in engaging in conversation. Yet as I got into the car, I felt the Lord bring to mind a truth about the driver: "He believes." So despite a bit of weariness, I began talking to him. After some chatting, I said to the young man, "It occurs to me that you are a believer."

He replied, "I am; how did you know?"

I told him that the Lord revealed it to me because God wanted to confirm his faith. Over the next forty minutes, because the Holy Spirit had confirmed my credibility with him, I was able to minister to and pray with him about his relationship with Jesus. He became a bold witness with his family who needed Jesus.

God understands that it can be uncomfortable to take a step of faith, such as speaking what you think you hear, much less being a witness for Christ. But He encourages and empowers you to push through. Remember the verse from chapter 7 encouraging you to set aside fear: "As we have been approved by God to be entrusted with the gospel, even so we speak, not as pleasing men, but God who tests our hearts" (1 Thessalonians 2:4). If you pray, listen, and then speak what the Holy Spirit prompts, it can open the doorway to another's heart. Speaking in faith can reveal and heal past or present conflicts and struggles and confirm God's activity in the other's life. There is often undeniable evidence that God is in the conversation.

Instant Conviction Leads to Instant Conversion

What would it be like if, as you witnessed to someone, both you and the person you were speaking with sensed the conviction that it was truly a divine moment—that God was present there in your midst, by virtue of what was being discussed? That's what we're talking about here. God has a great adventure for each of us to be able to experience as we step out in faith and are involved in conversations where it is strikingly obvious that it's a God moment. These adventures are waiting for us in the people we meet every day.

Scripture tells us that it is God's delight and purpose to convict others of their need for Him. Speaking of the Holy Spirit, Jesus said, "And when He has come, He will convict the world of sin, and of righteousness, and of judgment" (John 16:8). God desires to use you as an instrument to bring instant conviction to another's heart. After all, He knows all hearts intimately. You are called for this privilege. First Corinthians 14:24–25 affirms, "If all prophesy, and an unbeliever or an uninformed person comes in, he is convinced by all, he is convicted by all. And thus the secrets of his heart are revealed; and so, falling down on his face, he will worship God and report that God is truly among you."

The lost need a heart change.

Conviction of sin and a person's need for Jesus are essential to true conversion. Conviction leads to repentance. The lost need a heart change, not intellectual persuading. Sharing biblical truth, a unique word from the Holy Spirit, or even reciting God's law bridges the gap between the intellect and the heart and brings God's supernatural conviction.[5]

This is the biblical pattern of conversion modeled by Jesus Himself. Consider the story of the Samaritan woman at the well. She was deeply touched by the personal, supernaturally revealed knowledge Jesus spoke.[6] She was transformed from a woman of ill repute to a witness for Jesus who changed her city. This story is part of a larger pattern. Throughout Scripture, God's witnesses regularly relied on spiritually revealed knowledge to touch hearts. In many cases, there was no rational explanation for the origin of this knowledge. Because they were simply faithful to speak, many were convicted and their lives redeemed.

The Holy Spirit can use you in the same way! God will bring conviction, show you an opportunity, and open another's eyes to His reality and His involvement in your conversation if you are alert and receptive. I love to hear those I am witnessing to say, "How did you know that?" Speaking boldly is an adventure the Holy Spirit is inviting *you* into as well. When the other person senses something wonderful is happening, they will be open to the truth about their need for Jesus. You can be His tool to redeem, restore, and renew the hearts of those you meet. But you must pray, listen, and speak.

I encourage you, when you meet someone, to pray, "God, show me the door to their heart." Ask Him to open a door for witnessing. This is a common theme on sharing the gospel found throughout the New Testament: "I came to Troas to preach Christ's gospel, and a door was opened to me by the Lord" (2 Corinthians 2:12). Colossians 4:3 says, "Praying also for us, that God would open to us a door for the word, to speak the mystery of Christ, for which I am also in chains." And 1 Corinthians 16:9 affirms, "A great and effective door has opened to me."

Obedience, acting in *faith* by speaking what you believe, is from God. After all, "faith comes by hearing" (Romans 10:17). Faith is important in all of God's workings: "Without faith it is impossible to please Him, for he who comes to God must believe that He is, and that He is a rewarder of those who diligently seek Him" (Hebrews 11:6). You are rewarded when you are faithful!

When someone you are conversing with mentions something that stands out, or if a verse comes to your mind, have the bold faith to act by *speaking*. Intentionally make it a practice to be led by hearing from and *acting* on the promptings and conviction of the Holy Spirit. This kind of practice is biblical: "Solid food belongs to those who are of full age, that is, those who by reason of use have their senses exercised to discern both good and evil" (Hebrews 5:14). In addition, "as many as are led by the Spirit of God, these are sons of God" (Romans 8:14).

These verses mean the mature son or daughter of God develops a sense of discernment to determine what is good or evil in any situation. This is part of being led by the Holy Spirit. God encourages you to become proficient at using this "sense" of His leading—by practicing it. He made you for this! He has given you the ability to be led by the Holy Spirit into truth about another: "Lead me in Your truth and teach me, for You are the God of my salvation; on You I wait all the day" (Psalm 25:5). Friend, He created you for good works in Christ Jesus to bring increase to His kingdom. The finished work is what *God* does—not you. In the account above, I didn't convict the Uber driver's heart—God did that.

God says you are a minister of reconciliation (see 2 Corinthians 5:16–21). You are truly made for God's good work, so let Him do it! Many of us likely have sat through hundreds (some of us, thousands) of sermons and Bible studies. God can bring any of that to mind for His purpose in the moment of witnessing if you let Him.

God is with you as you move to lead another to Him. You are not doing this alone; the Holy Spirit is present to use your desire to evangelize for His glory. This is true joy! Psalm 16:11 says, "You will show me the path of life; in Your presence is fullness of joy; at Your right hand are pleasures forevermore." Along the path of life, you will encounter many whom God wants to reach and save. If you look and listen for that still small voice, then act on His prompting, you can experience the miraculous—and sense a deep joy in partnering with Him.

◆ ◆ ◆

Throughout this book we have discovered that the secret to hearing "well done" is to bring increase centered on the foundation of Jesus Christ. That means we must be participants in the gospel through our works. The good news is that God wants us to be wildly successful in sharing Jesus! He's made every provision through a partnership with His Holy Spirit in sharing.

This makes what can be a somewhat awkward-feeling practice of sharing your faith much easier. God has made sure you've got this! If you step out in faith to pray, listen, and speak, God will come through for you in the moment. Give Him the chance to be involved in your daily encounters with others. He is the One who carries the responsibility and weight of witnessing—not you. He destined you before the very foundation of the world to meet people along your path—and you may be the only Christian they ever meet. With the help of the Holy Spirit, you cannot fail when you speak in faith.

I have found that one of the "pinch points" in witnessing is speaking in a way that leads the conversation in a Godward direction. It may require a touch of intentionality, perhaps even a bit of boldness. At the point where you depart from day-to-day chitchat and steer onto a spiritual path, you may feel reluctance. This is normal, because talking about spirituality, including Jesus Christ, is not typical of our culture. The question is: Do you fear others more than God? "You shall not be afraid in any man's presence, for the judgment is God's" (Deuteronomy 1:17).

You must live in anticipation of eternity, when you will stand before the Lord. He may ask why you were fearful to share the good news about His Son. So be bold. Direct the conversation to the spiritual side, relying on the Holy Spirit to come through with what to say. Jesus said, "Do not worry beforehand, or premeditate what you will speak. But whatever is given you in that hour, speak that; for it is not you who speak, but the Holy Spirit" (Mark 13:11).

Depend on God when witnessing—not on what you know. You do not need to rely on your own knowledge to be an effective witness. The Bible counsels us to rely on the Holy Spirit's guidance. If you use discernment and speak what you discern, God can step in and touch the other person's heart. Depend on Him to provide the light; your job is to faithfully speak whatever God may want you to share.

As we close this chapter, I want to review what we have discussed. We've explored a *Bible-dependent strategy* as well as a *Holy Spirit–dependent strategy* to witnessing through the following steps:

1. Bible-Centered
Offer a gift to someone you meet whom God has laid on your heart to share with. Show them the index in the front of the Gideon New Testament, which addresses life's many problems and issues. Then show them the back of the book, which has the plan of salvation, the Romans Road. Let

them read that and ask what it means to them when they've finished reading each verse. Ask if they want to receive Christ as their Lord and Savior. Pray with them if they say yes.

2. Holy Spirit–Centered

Pray for wisdom and for the person's eyes to be opened. **Listen** with a receptive mind to what the Holy Spirit may be prompting in you. Be open to discernment regarding a verse or relevant comment mentioned. **Speak** with holy boldness what you sense God might be saying in this circumstance, not fearing what the other person might say.

3. The Most Important Step: Invite

The final and most important thing in witnessing is to *invite* the person if they believe in Christ's sacrifice and lordship. We will examine this step more closely in the next chapter, including practical examples to be successful. When you follow a biblical model for witnessing and the simple steps laid out in this chapter (offer a Bible or pray, listen, and speak), you can proclaim the truth boldly without fear. Sharing the gospel is the mandate and joy of every Christian's life, bringing increase for God's kingdom and qualifying us to hear the words "well done." Friend, you can begin today!

TIME	TO	GATE	REMARK
10:00	HEAVEN	A10	DELAYED
10:02	HEAVEN	A03	ON-TIME
10:08	HEAVEN	A06	CANCELED
10:09	HEAVEN	A12	ON-TIME
10:12	HEAVEN	B07	ON-TIME
10:14	HEAVEN	B02	DELAYED
10:21	HEAVEN	H07	ON-TIME

Prepare for Landing

I've noticed during my travels that when the flight attendant announces we will be landing soon, passengers begin to get a bit restless. I can understand the feeling. You've gone through all of the steps to board the plane, waited for several hours (depending on the duration of the flight), and now you're so close! But the time spent preparing to land is valuable. It is important that the captain remains focused and brings the plane down safely.

Similarly, it is important that when you are witnessing, you bring home the truth about Jesus. The final few moments of witnessing can be some of the most important. You need to continue praying throughout the conversation and allow the Spirit to finish the work God has begun in someone's life.

Remember Jason from the time-share booth? God revealed to me the very area of this man's heart where he was hurting the most. He was not wearing it on his countenance, but the Holy Spirit knew Jason's heart.

After Jason confessed to me that he was struggling in his faith, I responded, "Well, I'm just believing, Jason, that you want to return to the Lord. It seems to me that He probably sent me to ask if you want to rededicate your life right now to Jesus Christ." Tears welled up in his eyes as he said, "I sure would. Things are not working that well for me now." So with a heartfelt prayer, Jason gave his life back to Christ. This in itself is incredible! But the Holy Spirit was not finished working in Jason's life through our conversation.

As Jason was praying, another thought came to my mind: *His daughter is in danger.* This was a pretty wild thought, because he hadn't even told me whether he had a daughter, let alone about any danger. But I believed it was from the Lord, so after we prayed and he gave his life back to Jesus, I took the chance and boldly said, "You know, as you were praying, Jason, it occurred to me that your daughter might be in danger."

Once again, he looked astonished and asked, "How did you know that I have a daughter?"

I told him, "I don't, but I think the Lord revealed that to me." We prayed for God's protection over his daughter, and then I went into the gift shop at last to retrieve my family (and credit card).

About half an hour later I came out of the store with my family, and Jason wildly waved at me. I went over, and he excitedly exclaimed, "It wasn't even five minutes after we prayed for my daughter Justina's safety that she called me and said, 'Dad, I'm in trouble. I've been assigned to a group of other girls for the senior class by the guidance counselor at school, and they are all into drugs. Will you please do something to get me out of this situation?'"

It was clear to Jason at this point that the Holy Spirit personally and intimately met him that day. I affirmed this to him: "I believe the Lord is pleased that you rededicated your life to Him and wanted to show His approval and blessing on you and your family for this." You can trust that God will be faithful when you are bold to share!

What Will You Do to Have Your Best Life in Eternity?

1. Do you believe that conversion depends on God? How does this relieve some of your fears to share the gospel?

2. Reflect on the name El Chay, the Living God. In what ways have you seen this God show Himself alive in your life?

3. Is there one of the steps of effective witnessing that you tend to forget to do (pray, listen, speak, invite)? Which do you believe to be the most important, and why?

4. Consider the story of Jason and the information the Holy Spirit revealed. Have you had a similar experience? What do you see as the biblical role of the Holy Spirit?

5. What are some ways that you can practice discernment? Does this come easily to you, or is it an area you struggle with? How do you define being led by the Holy Spirit in your life?

6. Would you be willing to carry a pocket New Testament with you to share with someone else?

Chapter 10
The One-Week Challenge

We feel and know we are eternal.

—Spinoza

God created every person as immortal, in the sense that He destined your spirit to live forever. The question is *where* will you reside? One destination, heaven, is eternal bliss. The alternative is a place of eternal torment. Friend, each conversation that you have unfolds the opportunity to forever change another person's eternal destination. God has chosen His body, you and me, as champions for eternity's invitation. We see this in Scripture: "[God is] not willing that any should perish but that all should come to repentance" (2 Peter 3:9). God has chosen you as the gatekeeper in your sphere of influence. You are the vessel of His incredible eternal blessing and have the opportunity to pass it on to others! So what is holding you back? In this chapter, I want to deal with the final hurdle for you to overcome in witnessing. While you may tell your testimony and even share the gospel message, you may often leave out the last step: inviting the other person to accept Jesus.

And understandably so. This is the point where you can fear rejection or humiliation. You can be reluctant and feel like you are pushing your religion. However, the invitation is crucial—it is the point of decision. The eternal destiny of the person you speak with may hang in the balance of their acting on the truth you boldly share.

Remember, this is an exercise of faith. God's Word will do the convicting if you are faithful to put it in their hands. You can depend on the Holy Spirit to open their eyes by revealing the thoughts and intentions of their hearts. God can give you a verse that will sincerely touch the other. When that happens, inviting a response is a natural, easy, and logical next step.

On one of my trips, I was in an Uber car at 3 a.m., tired and wanting to rest on my ride home. Yet when I sat down, I asked the Lord, "Is there anything you would have me say to Chad, the driver?" A verse came to mind: "He who has the Son has life; he who does not have the Son of God does not have life" (1 John 5:12).

I spent a few minutes warming up to my driver and conversing with him in general terms. We then talked about his convictions. He told me that as a Black man, he had recently realized that he was conservative in his beliefs despite his upbringing and that it is important to live out one's convictions beyond tradition. This seemed like an open door for me to ask if he had any spiritual beliefs. He quickly replied, "I believe in a higher power."

I asked, "Do you think you have the hope of eternal life?"

Chad replied that he thought he did. We continued talking about God's holiness and humanity's sinfulness, yet he maintained that because he was a good guy, lived a good life, and had a belief in a higher power, he could probably make it to heaven.

I said, "Eternity is a pretty important thing to risk." I then used the verse that had come to my mind: "He who has the Son has life; he who does not have the Son of God does not have life."

This opened a woundedness in his heart, and he said, "You know, my uncle, who is just a little older than me, was a strong Christian man like you. I was mad at God for years when he died. But eventually I realized that dying is a part of living, and we all will die someday."

I said, "Yes, and Jesus Christ said that unless man is born again, he cannot see the kingdom of God."[1]

As we sat in my driveway, I used the opportunity to ask Chad if he wanted to receive Christ as his Savior and Lord. The invitation was an easy and natural outcome of the conversation we'd just had. The secrets of this man's heart—his woundedness about his uncle's death—had been wonderfully revealed by the Holy Spirit, which also brought about his subsequent conviction and my willingness to speak in faith.

When the Lord provides insight beyond your knowledge, you will have a new confidence that allows you to bring the conversation to a close. This process is an opportunity to strengthen your faith. In fact, I am convinced that inviting people to Jesus is the most important and neglected part of living the Christian life. If you have the holy boldness to *ask*, God can greatly use you to bring others to salvation.

You never know what is happening in another person's heart. It is easy to make assumptions based on their outward appearance or actions and conclude that they are far from accepting Jesus. But God knows the heart.

I remember when a young woman came into our pregnancy center and Kit, a counselor, met her at the window. Here is how Kit recounted the story:

> When I saw her, I immediately thought, *How in the world can I, a middle-aged woman, possibly relate to this girl?* She was plentifully tattooed and pierced in many

places. It seemed like there was a huge gap between us. To make matters worse, as I escorted her back to the counseling room, she said, "I want you to know I really don't want anything to do with your God and don't want to hear anything about your religion." So as we entered the room, I prayed, "God, if You're going to do anything here, if anything is going to happen, it is going to have to be totally You. Because I have nothing to offer this girl."

Yet as we conversed over the next hour, the Lord opened up insight into her heart. I was able to bring up spiritual matters and direct the conversation to the gospel of Jesus Christ. And to my utter surprise, when I asked if she wanted to receive Him as her Lord and Savior today, she resoundingly said, "Yes, I would."

I learned a lesson that day about God's sovereignty, His wisdom, and His power to change hearts that I never knew before. What I thought was impossible was, in fact, God's perfect opportunity for this girl to become a follower of Jesus.

Friend, your job is not to judge whether another person is ready to receive the gospel but to be faithful to share—and let the Holy Spirit do the rest. You will be eternally rewarded when you do! This is the point where you most often panic. You hesitate just short of the finish line, of actually asking others to act on the life-giving truth of the gospel. Why?

This is the point of life or death—truly. Somehow, deep within yourself, you sense this. Maybe it is the critical nature of the moment that causes you to pause. It could be a reluctance to fail. In chapter 8, we examined obstacles to successful witnessing. Most of our reluctances to share are founded in self-protection. We are afraid of embarrassment or rejection.

Whatever the hindrance, you must—in faith—step forward boldly and ask for a commitment. As we have read, heaven offers eternal rewards for the increase you bring! It also is your delightful duty. Scripture calls for those responsible for others (that's you and I!) to sound a clear call: "For if the trumpet makes an uncertain sound, who will prepare for battle?" (1 Corinthians 14:8). Ezekiel 33:6 says, "If the watchman sees the sword coming and does not blow the trumpet, and the people are not warned, and the sword comes and takes any person from among them, he is taken away in his iniquity; but his blood I will require at the watchman's hand."

The watchman's responsibility is yours as well. You have knowledge of eternity (the risk of separation from God), and you are obligated to share the message with others. While I doubt that God will hold you directly responsible for those you witness to who remain unsaved, I am certain He wants you to give a clear invitation to come drink deeply of the gift of eternal life: "Ho! Everyone who thirsts, come to the waters; and you who have no money, come, buy and eat. . . . Eat what is good, and let your soul delight itself in abundance" (Isaiah 55:1–2).

This invitation to abundant life is not from you—it is, in fact, God who is inviting others to delight in Him. He is inviting them to life instead of death, to eternal peace instead of everlasting torment, to light instead of darkness, to heaven instead of hell. This is the good news of salvation! You may have heard the expression "don't shoot me, I am just the messenger." That is you—just a messenger: "This is the message which we have heard from Him and declare to you, that God is light and in Him is no darkness at all" (1 John 1:5). You are an appointed ambassador of the sovereign country of heaven! You are sent to bring an invitation from the nation's great King: Come to that kingdom and enjoy eternal life—come live forever! Second

Corinthians 5:20 tells us, "Now then, we are ambassadors for Christ, as though God were pleading through us: we implore you on Christ's behalf, be reconciled to God." Inviting another to Jesus is the most exciting endeavor you could possibly be involved with.

Someone you know or meet may never make it to heaven without you telling them about Jesus. Don't withhold this knowledge from them!

The King of life has given you the key to eternal life to share with them. John 10:28 says, "I give them eternal life, and they shall never perish; neither shall anyone snatch them out of My hand." And John 17:3 affirms, "This is eternal life, that they may know You, the only true God, and Jesus Christ whom You have sent."

Jesus paid their admission price for entrance into eternal life: "Christ also suffered once for sins, the just for the unjust, that He might bring us to God, being put to death in the flesh but made alive by the Spirit" (1 Peter 3:18).

God will be with you, in the person of the Holy Spirit, and help you to know what to say in that hour and conversation. John 14:16–18 says, "I will pray the Father, and He will give you another Helper, that He may abide with you forever—the Spirit of truth . . . I will not leave you orphans; I will come to you." Luke 12:12 reminds us, "The Holy Spirit will teach you in that very hour what you ought to say."

All you have to do is be faithful to ask others if they believe and wish to accept God's gift. Speak the Word boldly. Second Corinthians 5:19 promises, "That is, that God was in Christ reconciling the world to Himself, not imputing their trespasses to them, and has committed to us the word of reconciliation".

The invitation to accept Christ makes all the difference. I recently expressed the importance of this step to a pregnancy ministry in Florida. Here is what the director said a few months later: "Last year we saw twenty women receive Jesus Christ as Lord. Since then, we are being intentional about sharing an invitation to receive Jesus. We have seen forty-three women in only six months. The number has more than doubled!"

In presenting the life, death, and resurrection of Jesus, you have the privilege of inviting others to *act on* these facts personally. In doing so, they will live forever—and you will be able to say to our Lord, "You delivered to me five talents; look, I have gained five more talents" (Matthew 25:20).

Friend, if you hope to hear the words "well done, good and faithful servant" and experience heaven's best rewards, you must be willing to share the entire gospel. You must invite the other person to accept Jesus Christ as their Savior. We see this in the Great Commission, where Jesus said,

> "All authority has been given to Me in heaven and on earth. Go therefore and make disciples of all the nations, baptizing them in the name of the Father and of the Son and of the Holy Spirit, teaching them to observe all things that I have commanded you; and lo, I am with you always, even to the end of the age" (Matthew 28:18–20).

As the leader of a ministry in which thousands come to Christ, the question I am often asked by supporters is "How are you discipling the converts?" This question is especially important in light of the Great Commission. We are to make disciples! Yet I have found that the responsibility and importance of the initial witness are often discounted. The mandate to make disciples is a mandate to take the first step and make converts. In fact, the emphasis on disciple-making often misses a seemingly obvious fact: 100 percent

> **Conversion is the first step in discipleship.**

of every disciple made must first be a convert. Conversion is the first step in discipleship. No conversion, no acceptance of Christ's salvation and lordship, means no disciples.

You must lead others to Christ, since being born again is the first step. If you want to hear the words "well done" and fulfill the Great Commission, you must witness. This is bringing true increase with our lives, each one of us—not just the missionaries, pastors, or professional Christians only, but you and me as well.

Together we have looked at two God-dependent, Bible-based strategies to witnessing. These strategies are God-led, not based on memory, questions, or our ability. They use Scripture and the Holy Spirit's leading to intimately and powerfully touch the heart of the lost coworker or family member in our life.

We also have examined the many fears and hindrances that distract us from bringing true increase—people being saved—in our Christian walk. In this closing chapter I offer you a simple challenge. I personally invite you to fulfill the Great Commission in your life, beginning today.

The One-Week Challenge

God is urgent about everyone coming to Christ. We see this in 2 Corinthians 6:2, which says, "For He says: 'In an acceptable time I have heard you, and in the day of salvation I have helped you.' Behold, now is the accepted time; behold, now is the day of salvation." Now is the time; *today* is the day of salvation. This is the essence of the one-week challenge. Are you willing to step into the most exciting journey of your life?

If God were to send a person across your path *this week*, would you be willing to witness to them? Are you willing to commit to doing this before the Lord? Would you pray, "God, if You send a person to me this week whom I could witness to and invite to Jesus, I will be faithful to do it"?

I invite you to consider this challenge as from the Lord.

After all, the Great Commission is applicable to everyone; it is God's challenge to you. It is His command to be obeyed. So let's get practical here. Make the commitment to witness to the next person God sends your way—and be on the alert for the encounter this week. It might be the guy who sits next to you on the bus, a coworker in the lunchroom, an old friend who calls, or your child or parent. Be alert to the opportunity and take it as God's answer to your prayer. Are you willing to take the step of faith and ask your Father to send someone to you this week? When He does, move confidently into the conversation. You never know how close the person may be to surrendering to Jesus Christ—unless you ask, "Do you sense God is wanting you to make a commitment to Jesus today?" You will be surprised how many will say yes, so be ready to ask. "Preach the word! Be ready in season and out of season. Convince, rebuke, exhort, with all longsuffering and teaching" (2 Timothy 4:2).

Scripture urges us to be bold and speak, whether it is convenient or not. Use God's Word to instruct and deal with the needs of the person before you. Do so with bold gentleness in consideration of the magnitude of the moment. After all, their eternal destiny may be in question. "Sanctify the Lord God in your hearts, and always be ready to give a defense to everyone who asks you a reason for the hope that is in you, with meekness and fear" (1 Peter 3:15).

Again, I encourage you to be ready for the Lord to send someone to you. Be alert. It may be someone whose heart He has been working on already. Be faithful to sow the seed of the gospel in their heart:

> A sower went out to sow his seed. And as he sowed, some fell by the wayside; and it was trampled down, and the birds of the air devoured it. Some fell on rock; and as soon as it sprang up, it withered away because it lacked

moisture. And some fell among thorns, and the thorns sprang up with it and choked it. But others fell on good ground, sprang up, and yielded a crop a hundredfold. (Luke 8:5–8)

Remember, God is not looking for talented evangelists or super-Christians. Friend, you already have what it takes to witness effectively! God is simply looking for FAT believers.

Faithful to sow the seed of the good news and trust God with the outcome.
Available regardless of the convenience of the circumstance.
Teachable and humble enough to be led by the Holy Spirit in every situation.

As an ambassador and emissary of the King, you can show others heaven's door: "Jesus said to them again, 'Most assuredly, I say to you, I am the door of the sheep'" (John 10:7). Each man or woman is a wanderer needing direction to the path of eternal life. You have found that way: "Jesus said to him, 'I am *the way*, the truth, and the life. No one comes to the Father except through Me'" (John 14:6, emphasis mine). Share this truth with them!

The next person you meet this week may have an inward spiritual thirst and a need for the *water* of life. You have drunk deeply of it—offer for them to come and drink of this cup: "The Spirit and the bride say, 'Come!' And let him who hears say, 'Come!' And let him who thirsts come. Whoever desires, let him take the water of life freely" (Revelation 22:17). In John 4:14 Jesus said, "Whoever drinks of the water that I shall give him will never thirst. But the water that I shall give him will become in him a fountain of water springing up into everlasting life."

The next person you meet may perish if they do not take of the *bread* of heaven; offer them Jesus: "Jesus said to them, 'I am the bread of life. He who comes to Me shall never hunger, and he who believes in Me shall never thirst'" (John 6:35). And John 6:33 says, "The bread of God is He who comes down from heaven and gives life to the world."

Take this challenge personally. Believe that God Himself can direct a person to you—a person you are uniquely qualified to share with, who needs Jesus. You can seize the joyful privilege of sharing the precious treasure of heaven, the gospel, with them . . . this week.

This is why the master said, "Well done, good and faithful servant." In chapter 1, we saw that the first two stewards used the talents the master gave them for the intended purpose: to bring *increase*. The good news of Jesus is not another twenty-first-century sound bite that you hear and file away like the evening news. It is the very gift of eternal life! The Word says the race before you must be completed: "Do you not know that those who run in a race all run, but one receives the prize? Run in such a way that you may obtain it" (1 Corinthians 9:24). Are you winning others to Jesus?

Impact on a Church

Has the church you attend ever publicly committed to share Jesus? I taught this simple strategy on a Sunday morning at The Blended Church in Indianapolis where I am a member. The sermon was about the topics examined in this book. The one-week challenge was given to the congregation, and I extended the following call to the church: "How many of you would be willing to say to God, 'If You will send someone into my life this week, I will be faithful to share Jesus with them'?" Then we asked for a commitment by a show of raised hands. Eight hundred of the thousand people present raised their hands and committed to share Jesus with someone *that week*. Then a card (see pages 236-239) was handed out to everyone who had volunteered.

What happened the following Sunday was encouraging. People came to me stating that they had shared the Lord with a relative or friend who accepted Christ. A Sunday school teacher said he had taught the gospel for weeks but never invited the class to *act* on the gospel; ten boys gave their hearts to Jesus when he asked—and the teacher made sure they were sincere. A man said that both of his brothers came to Christ. For weeks afterward, the pastor emphasized evangelism and practiced it himself. Many were saved. Here is how one of the pastors responded.

> **Has your church ever publicly challenged members to share Jesus?**

Hello, Dan,

I wanted to follow up on our conversation in writing to further explain the impact your message had on our congregation. I am in a pretty unique position at the church in that I have more contact with congregation members than most of our pastors. In my meetings with them I often get to hear the impact a particular message had or is having on their life.

I can say with no hesitation that your evangelism message had quite the impact on several members in our church. A few I met with stated that your message reminded them why we should and how to get "past" or "over" themselves to do what God has called us all to do. I personally witnessed attendees going from a place of "I can't" to "I have to do this and have been empowered to do so!"

I could go on about some of the awesome results that came of that message, but I am most grateful that you submitted to what God had to say and did a great job acting as HIS mouthpiece.

A Question for Leaders

Has there been a time when the church you attend made a public commitment to share Jesus with another person—ever, let alone to share *that week*? It seems a bit like the gift of the obvious that a congregation should be committed to sharing the gospel; this is, after all, God's commission to His church.

How about your church? How about you personally? Will you accept this challenge and bring increase for that day when you stand in eternity? Will the Lord be able to say, because of the increase you brought with your church or life, "Well done, good and faithful servant. Enter into the joy of your lord"?

The church is a hospital for the wounded and broken, a school to equip disciples, and a family and home for the Christ-follower. While never neglecting these aspects of church life, each believer, deacon, elder, and minister's heart should also be burdened by these questions:

1. What is the emphasis given to the gospel in my church?
2. How well does my church equip and encourage believers to share Jesus with others?
3. What place does the Great Commission have in my church?

It is a matter of perspective. We, as the church and as individuals, need to understand who and Whose we are. We walk in communion with, carry the mandate from, and possess the authority of the awesome King of heaven. Virtually everyone we meet—from the common individual to the most prestigious leader—is the same. Each is in desperate need of salvation. We have the answer to that need. Being faithful throughout life to this daily call will certainly motivate Jesus to say to you that which we all long to hear:

"Well done, good and faithful servant. Enter into the joy of your master"(ESV).

TIME	TO	GATE	REMARK
10:00	HEAVEN	A10	DELAYED
10:02	HEAVEN	A03	ON-TIME
10:08	HEAVEN	A06	CANCELED
10:09	HEAVEN	A12	ON-TIME
10:12	HEAVEN	B07	ON-TIME
10:14	HEAVEN	B02	DELAYED
10:21	HEAVEN	H07	ON-TIME

Final Destination

The moment of stepping off the plane and having arrived at your destination is the best part of traveling. It is the relief of safely arriving where you intended and, if you are on vacation, the anticipation of the plans and pleasures that are yet to come. But none of this compares to the joy you will feel upon entering the presence of God in heaven, your final destination, and hearing Him welcome you with the affirmation of "well done, good and faithful servant." In this life, God gives small glimpses of eternity to remind you of His goodness and the rewards awaiting those who are faithful to bring increase.

I experienced the goodness of God's presence in a wonderful way while in a state park with my daughters on a Sunday. I had prayed that morning, "Lord, I have not had a decent chance to witness to someone this week." (As a sidenote, my New Year's resolution is to share the gospel with someone once per week, or fifty-two times this year.) The afternoon of that morning prayer, we pulled off the road to climb an observation tower in the park.

The day was waning, and most of the people had left the park by that time. We were fairly alone. I noticed, however, that there was a truck parked in front of the observation tower—obviously someone else was enjoying the view.

As we ascended the steps of the tower, the view before us showed undulating hills for seemingly endless miles of green. It was gorgeous. There, enjoying the scenery with us, was a young man in his twenties. I prayed, "Lord, would You have me witness to this guy, and if so, what would You have me say?" A thought came to mind: *This man is in love with nature.*

My daughters and I engaged him in about half an hour of conversation, and I commented, "It seems to me that you're deeply in love with nature."

He seemed surprised and said, "Yes, it's Sunday, and I have kind of a Buddhist spirituality that this is my god." He waved his hands over the terrain before us.

I said, "The Lord Jesus Christ is the One who told me that you're in love with nature because He is the One who made nature and who made you. He just wants you to know that He loves you so much that He'd rather die than live without you. In fact, He did that for you on the cross." I went on to share the gospel with him. Then we prayed together, and he accepted Jesus as his Savior. It was a small moment of eternal significance as we looked out on the beauty of the hills that God had created.

Simply, I had faith to believe the young man's presence

there in the tower was God's answer to my prayer to witness to somebody that week. Choosing to listen to the Holy Spirit and then share led to God meeting this man in the park that afternoon. In the same way, God wants to send someone into your life to give you the opportunity to share your hope of salvation . . . this week. In doing so, you will store up treasure in heaven, bring Christ-centered increase with your life, and have confidence that you will hear Jesus tell you, "Well done." He longs for you to step into your high and holy calling as an ambassador of heaven, to use you for eternity with someone you meet today. Will you let Him?

What Will You Do to Have Your Best Life in Eternity?

1. How does the reality that each person in your life will live forever in heaven or hell affect your intentionality to share Christ?

2. In this world, ambassadors to another country have responsibilities. What do you see as your responsibilities as an ambassador of Jesus Christ's kingdom?

3. Are you willing to try the Bible-centered or Spirit-centered approach to witnessing this week?

4. Imagine for a moment standing before Jesus and Him commending you for introducing somebody to Him through sharing the gospel. What would that be like?

5. Are you willing to boldly believe that the next person you encounter may be a divine appointment by God, for you to share the key for them to live forever? Are you willing to share Jesus with another this week to act out the Great Commission and secure the likelihood that Jesus will tell you, "Well done," and make you eligible for the vast rewards He has for those who overcome?

6. Does your church actively encourage and mentor believers to share Jesus with others?

Acknowledgments

All glory, honor, and praise to the CEO of PreBorn! and of my life, who commissioned this book: Jesus the Messiah!

To the most precious women in my life:

My wife, Valerie Kay Steiner
My daughter with Jesus, Grace Nicole Steiner
My daughters Naomi and Jessica, whom I was with less frequently in writing
My daughter Misty, whose faith is an inspiration
My beloved mother, Frieda May Steiner, whose works remain unpublished

Thanks are due to the Board of Directors at PreBorn! who love the gospel and embrace the concept of this book and its distribution.

Endnotes

Chapter 1
1. To learn more about what a calling is and how to identify yours, I recommend William W. Klein's *What Is My Calling?: A Biblical and Theological Exploration of Christian Identity* (Grand Rapids, MI: Baker Books, 2022).
2. Rev. Frederick W. Robertson, *Sermons Preached at Brighton* (New York: Harper & Brothers, 1872), 341.
3. See Galatians 5:19–23.

Chapter 2
1. For further reading, check out Randy Alcorn's book *Heaven: A Comprehensive Guide to Everything the Bible Says About Our Eternal Home* (Wheaton, IL: Tyndale, 2004).
2. Harvest Ministries with Greg Laurie, PO Box 4000, Riverside, CA, 92514.
3. Bruce Wilkinson, *The Prayer of Jabez*, The Breakthrough Series (Sisters, OR: Multnomah Publishers, 2000), 39.
4. Wilkinson, *The Prayer of Jabez*, 23.
5. Mark Giszczak, "Two Ways to Calculate the Value of a Talent," Catholic Bible Student, January 27, 2022, https://catholicbiblestudent.com/2022/01/two-ways-to-calculate-the-value-of-a-talent.html.
6. James Strong, s.v. "kurios (n.)," in *Strong's Expanded Exhaustive Concordance of the Bible* (Nashville: Thomas Nelson, 2009), https://biblehub.com/greek/2962.htm.
7. Rev. Ron Godbolt, "Master Has Many Names with Same Meaning," *Fayetteville Observer*, January 16, 2019, https://www.fayobserver.com/story/lifestyle/faith/2019/01/16/rev-ron-Godbolt-master-has-many-names-with-same-meaning/6283166007/.
8. Don Stewart, "What Does the Greek Word Kurios (Lord) Mean?," Blue Letter Bible, accessed December 3, 2023, https://www.blueletterbible.org/faq/don_stewart/don_stewart_1307.cfm.
9. "What will our rewards in the Kingdom be?," Verse by Verse Ministry, accessed June 17, 2024, https://versebyverseministry.org/bible-answers/explaining-talents-vs-minas?locale=en.

Chapter 3
1. (Galatians 5:22–23) The fruit of the Spirit is love, joy, peace, longsuffering, kindness, goodness, faithfulness, gentleness, self-control.

2. For more information on the great white throne and judgment seat, see https://www.blueletterbible.org/faq/don_stewart/don_stewart_146.cfm and https://www.blueletterbible.org/faq/don_stewart/don_stewart_144.cfm.
3. Excerpt from Mike Goeke, "God Uses Heat to Refine Us, Show His Reflection in Us,"*Midland Reporter-Telegram*, May 25, 2011, https://www.mrt.com/lifestyles/religion/article/God-uses-heat-to-refine-us-show-his-reflection-7438400.php.

Chapter 4
1. John McRay, s.v. "Saints (n.)," in Bible Study Tools, accessed December 3, 2023, https://www.biblestudytools.com/dictionary/saints/.
2. See Revelation 2:11; 20:6, 14; and 21:8.
3. See Exodus 16.
4. Ron Meacock, "White Stone," Tellout.com, 2021, https://www.tellout.com/revelation/now11.htm.
5. James Strong, s.v. "kainos (adj.)," in *Strong's Expanded Exhaustive Concordance of the Bible* (Nashville: Thomas Nelson, 2009), https://biblehub.com/greek/2537.htm.
6. See also Revelation 19:8, 14.
7. See Revelation 17:8; 20:15.
8. See Matthew 19:28 and Luke 22:30.
9. See Matthew 25:34–35 and Galatians 4:7.
10. Although Scripture uses a male pronoun here, we are all included in this promise.
11. See 2 Samuel 11.

Chapter 5
1. James Strong, s.v. "nikaó (v.)," in *Strong's Expanded Exhaustive Concordance of the Bible* (Nashville: Thomas Nelson, 2009), https://biblehub.com/greek/3528.htm.
2. Strong, s.v. "hēttōntai (v.)," in *Strong's Expanded Exhaustive Concordance of the Bible*, https://biblehub.com/greek/he_tto_ntai_2274.htm.
3. Paul's conversion story can be found in Acts 9.
4. See Joshua 6.
5. Peter Colón, "How Big Is How Big Is Your God," *Israel My Glory* (January/February 2004), https://israelmyglory.org/article/how-big-is-how-big-is-your-God/.
6. Bryant G. Wood, "The Walls of Jericho," Associates for Biblical Research, June 9, 2008, https://biblearchaeology.org/research/conquest-of-canaan/3625-the-walls-of-jericho.

7. Strong, s.v. "kosmos (n.)," in *Strong's Expanded Exhaustive Concordance of the Bible*, https://biblehub.com/greek/2889.htm.

Chapter 6
1. "Public Sees Religion's Influence Waning," Pew Research Center, September 22, 2014, https://www.pewresearch.org/religion/2014/09/22/public-sees-religions-influence-waning-2/.
2. Widely attributed to Margaret Mead.
3. "How Much Do You Tithe at Church?," Ministry Designs, accessed December 3, 2023, https://ministrydesigns.com/how-much-do-you-tithe-at-church/.
4. James Strong, s.v. "paraklétos (n.)," in *Strong's Expanded Exhaustive Concordance of the Bible* (Nashville: Thomas Nelson, 2009), https://biblehub.com/greek/3875.htm.
5. Costi Hinn, "The Romans Road to Salvation," For the Gospel, accessed December 3, 2023, https://www.forthegospel.org/read/the-romans-road-to-salvation.

Chapter 7
1. Dan Gummel, "What Does the Word 'Gospel' Mean?," *BibleProject Podcast*, Bible Project, September 9, 2019, https://bibleproject.com/podcast/what-does-word-gospel-mean/.
2. See https://evangelismexplosion.org/resources/steps-to-life/.

Chapter 8
1. James Strong, s.v. "epaischunomai (v.)," in *Strong's Expanded Exhaustive Concordance of the Bible* (Nashville: Thomas Nelson, 2009), https://biblehub.com/greek/1870.htm.
2. See Psalm 37:23.
3. "Evangelism for Dummies," *Relevant*, February 26, 2002, https://relevantmagazine.com/faith/163-evangelism-for-dummies/.
4. Samuel Butler, *Hudibras in Three Parts,* Part 3, Canto III (London: W. Rogers, 1684), 202 (Early English Books Online 2, ProQuest).
5. See Acts 26.
6. James Faris, "The Most Frequent Command in the Bible: Do Not Be Afraid," Core Christianity, November 27, 2019, https://corechristianity.com/resource-library/articles/the-most-frequent-command-in-the-bible-do-not-be-afraid/.

Chapter 9
1. See 1 Samuel 16:1–13.
2. Costi Hinn, "The Romans Road to Salvation," For the Gospel,

accessed December 3, 2023, https://www.forthegospel.org/read/the-romans-road-to-salvation.
3. "El Chay—The Living God," Inspired, October 2, 2008, https://mbentham.wordpress.com/2008/10/02/el-chay-the-living-god/.
4. Hinn, "Romans Road," https://www.forthegospel.org/read/the-romans-road-to-salvation.
5. Ray Comfort, "You Must Use the Law in Evangelism," Living Waters, April 29, 2021, https://livingwaters.com/you-must-use-the-law-in-evangelism/.
6. See John 4:16–18, 29.

Chapter 10
1. See John 3:3.

About the Author

As a visionary leader under the direction of Jesus Christ, Dan has led ministry characterized by unique entrepreneurial innovation in the not-for-profit arena.

He serves as founder and Chair of PreBorn! Under his leadership, PreBorn! has grown into the single most successful pro-life mission in the world, seeing over 80,000 commitments to Christ. Known for championing the gospel, he has worked alongside nationally recognized personalities like Glenn Beck, Ben Shapiro, Charlie Kirk, Candace Owens, Tucker Carlson, and Dan Bongino. Together, Dan and his wife, Valerie, have five children and nine grandchildren, and they reside in Indianapolis, Indiana.

Practical tools for evangelism

There is no greater way to hear the words "well done good and faithful servant," than to practically apply what you have learned and share your great love for your Master and Lord Jesus Christ to other people, by sharing the gospel of Jesus.

Here are some resources to help you on that journey!

Share Jesus Without Fear—(lifeway.com/en/product-family/share-jesus-without-fear): this resource from Lifeway is a very effective way to leads someone to Christ through them reading the scripture themselves. The site has a leader›s guide Bible study book and witnessing cards.

The Romans Road—(bible.org/illustration/romans-road): A quick, effective and common evangelism outline to use in sharing.

The Gideons International—(https://www.gideons.org/): discounted and highly effective New Testaments with the scriptural planned of salvation in all languages, as an evangelism tool to all members. Please get me a graphic of an open Bible that we can use have permission and

The Jesus film project app—(jesusfilm.org/tools/app): A full digital library of more than 200 full length movies and short films to help the world know Jesus better in their own language

Evangelism Explosion International (https://evangelismexplosion.org/resources/): training for yourself or your congregation on how to share the gospel through your testimony. The site also includes witnessing tips and the power of your story.

Billy Graham—(https://billygraham.org/grow-your-faith/how-to-share-your-faith/tools/): A resource library full of both free and paid resources to help equip you for sharing the gospel.

Living Waters—(Livingwaters.com): a ministry by ray comfort with a multitude of evangelism resources and films on how to personally share your faith-based on the law of God.

Cru—(cru.org/us/en/train-and-grow/share-the-gospel/personal-evangelism-101.html): Personal evangelism 101 the complete guide. A website that guide you through content on preparing and engaging in personal evangelism with tips

Navigators—(https://www.navigators.org/resource/one-verse-evangelism/): One Verse Evangelism: A simple, interactive way to share Christ conversationally and visually with the bridge illustration using Romans 6:23.

North America mission Board—(https://www.namb.net/evangelism/): evangelism resource catalog.

SHARE JESUS WITHOUT FEAR*

the invitation

TRUTHS

"By grace you are saved through faith, and this is not from yourselves." Ephesians 2:8

"And I was with you in weakness and in fear and much trembling, and my speech and my message were not in plausible words of wisdom, but in demonstration of the Spirit and of power." 1 Corinthians 2:3-4

"No one can come to Me unless the Father who sent Me draws him." John 6:44

"We are ambassadors for Christ; certain that God is appealing through us, we plead on Christ's behalf, 'Be reconciled to God.'" 2 Corinthians 5:20

"My word ... will not return to Me empty." Isaiah 55:11

"Go, therefore, and make disciples of all nations." Matthew 28:19

SHARE WITHOUT FEAR

How often have you wanted to share your faith but were afraid of failing? Success is more than just leading someone to Christ.

SUCCESS IN WITNESSING COMES FROM LIVING THE CHRISTIAN LIFE DAILY, SHARING THE GOSPEL, AND TRUSTING GOD FOR THE RESULTS.

PRINCIPLE

GOD DOES THE WORK.

WE CANNOT FAIL.

IT IS ALL GOD'S WORK.

More from Without Fear Witnessing Guides. © 1997 Lifeway Press. Item 54092-9732. *Printed in the USA. Scripture quotations are taken from The Holy Bible, English Standard Version® ESV. Copyright © 2001 by Crossway, a publishing ministry of Good News Publishers. All rights reserved.*

1. USE QUESTIONS THAT SHOW WHERE GOD IS WORKING

1. What are your spiritual beliefs?
2. Who is Jesus, to you?
3. Do you believe there is a heaven and a hell?
4. If you were to die, where would you go?
5. If what you believe is false, would you want to know it?

2. LET THE BIBLE DO THE WORK
As you read the verse aloud, ask "What does this say to you?"

1. "For all have sinned." Romans 3:23
2. "For the wages of sin is death." Romans 6:23
3. "Jesus answered him, 'Truly, truly, I say to you, unless one is born again he cannot see the kingdom of God.'" John 3:3
4. "I am the way." John 14:6
5. "If you confess with your mouth that Jesus is Lord and believe in your heart that God raised him from the dead, you will be saved." Romans 10:9-11
6. "Those who live might no longer live for themselves." 2 Corinthians 5:15
7. "I am the door. If anyone enters by me, he will be saved" John 10:9

3. FINISH WITH CRUCIAL QUESTIONS

1. Are you a sinner?
2. Do you want to be forgiven for your sins?
3. Do you believe Jesus died on the cross for you and rose again?
4. Are you ready to surrender your life to Christ?
5. Are you prepared to let Jesus into your life and into your heart?

After asking question 5, be silent and pray.

Salvation Prayer

Heavenly Father, I have sinned against You. I repent and humbly ask for your forgiveness from all of my sins. I believe Jesus died on the cross for me and rose again the third day. Father, I give You control of my life, make me into a new creation just as you promise. I accept Jesus Christ as my Lord and my Savior. Today is the day of my Salvation and I will strive to live a life honoring to You. I ask all these things in the Name of your Son and my Savior, Jesus Christ. Amen.

the invitation

SIN - THE PROBLEM

All have sinned. Romans 3:23
The wages of sin is death. Romans 6:23

SOLUTION - JESUS

I am The Way. John 14:6
You must be born again. John 3:3
If you confess you will be saved. Romans 10: 9-11

SALVATION - FAITH

No longer live for themselves. 2 Corinthians 5:15
I stand at the door and knock. Revelation 3:20

PreBorn!
preborn.com

Made in the USA
Monee, IL
24 October 2024